DrawPlus X6 User Guide

Contents

1. Welcome 1
   - Welcome 3
   - New features 3
   - Installation 6

2. Getting Started 9
   - Startup Wizard 11
   - Starting with a new drawing 12
   - Opening a drawing 15
   - Saving your work 16

3. Pages 17
   - Using the page and pasteboard 19
   - Setting measurement units and drawing scale 20
   - Viewing pages 23
   - Adding and deleting pages 24

4. Lines, Curves, and Shapes 25

Selecting one or more objects 27
Drawing lines and shapes 29
Using QuickShapes 35
Drawing spirals 37
Drawing arcs 39
Drawing triangles 41
Editing lines and shapes 43
Converting a shape to editable curves 49
Connectors 50
Adding dimension lines and labels 54
Using the Gallery 57

5. Using Brushes 59

Selecting brushes 61
Applying brush strokes 63
Pressure sensitivity 65

6. Text 67

Entering text 69
Editing text 70
Using fonts 73
Fitting text to a path 74

Contents

7. Manipulating Objects 75

- Copying, pasting, cutting, and deleting objects 77
- Cloning an object 78
- Copying an object's formatting 80
- Moving objects 81
- Resizing objects 81
- Rotating and shearing objects 83
- Cutting up objects 85
- Erasing and adding to objects 87
- Joining objects 88

8. Arranging Objects 91

- Grouping objects 93
- Aligning and distributing objects 94
- Ordering objects 95
- Working with layers 96

9. Fills, Lines, Colours, and Transparency 101

- Setting fill properties 103
- Setting line properties 109
- Sampling colours 112
- Defining line and fill colours 114
- Working with gradient fills 116
- Working with bitmap and plasma fills 120
- Working with mesh fills 121
- Understanding blend modes 123
- Setting opacity 124
- Using transparency effects 127

10. Pictures 131

    Importing pictures...133
    Using Cutout Studio 134
    Autotracing 136
    Applying PhotoLab filters 139

11. Effects 143

    Using graphic styles..145
    Applying 2D filter effects 149
    Applying 3D filter effects 151
    Adding drop shadows...153
    Creating blends 155
    Applying perspective 157
    Applying envelopes 158
    Using stencils..159

12. Stopframe/Keyframe Animation 163

    Getting started with animation 165
    Working with Stopframe animation 166
    Working with Keyframe animation 168
    Keyframe object control 173
    Joints 176
    Exporting animations 180

13. Publishing and Exporting 183

    Interactive Print/PDF Preview 185
    Printing basics 187
    Publishing as PDF 189
    Exporting objects and drawings 191

14. Additional Information 199
Contacting Serif 201
Credits 202

15. Index 205

1 Welcome

Welcome

Welcome to **DrawPlus X6**—the design and illustration solution from **Serif**, packed with all the features expected of award-winning design software. From **decorative page elements** and **logos** to **full-page illustrations**, **scale drawings**, **multi-page folded publications**, and **Stopframe** or **Keyframe animations**—DrawPlus X6 does it all. With the power of scalable vector graphics at your command, you'll see the creative possibilities open up right before your eyes! Whether you're a beginner or an expert, you'll find easy-to-use tools you can use right away.

If you've upgraded from a previous version, this new edition of DrawPlus includes a host of exciting new features which complement DrawPlus's existing features. We hope you also enjoy the additional power and performance edge.

Don't forget to register your new copy, using the **Registration Wizard** on the **Help** menu. That way, we can keep you informed of new developments and future upgrades!

New features

- **64-bit operation**
  DrawPlus is fully optimized for operation on 64-bit computers, and will automatically install for 64-bit operation accordingly.

Creative

- **Add impact with a ready-to-go stencil** (see p. 159)
  The **Stencils tab** provides a selection of ready-to-go stencil templates—all designed with the DrawPlus user in mind. Simply drag and drop your chosen stencil onto your page, then paint over it with the **Brush Tool**, or use it to cut out a design from a picture. You can even create your own stencils from shapes.

- **Drawing arcs is easy!** (see p. 39)
  The Arc Tool lets you create convex and concave arcs in your drawing, either as closed shapes or arc lines. Creating arcs using more complex curve drawing is now avoided.

- **Create spirals** (see p. 37)
  The **Spiral Tool** lets you add simple spiral shapes with powerful as-you-draw controls—flip or change spiral length/spacing with ease. Any spiral, being line-based, can take any line/fill property or brush stroke!

- **Draw adjustable triangles simply** (see p. 41)
  Use the **Triangle Tool** for both equilateral and isosceles triangles. Once drawn, drag corner nodes to make scalene triangles.

- **Generate palettes from pictures** (see p. 116)
  The new **Palette Creator** intelligently and automatically "extracts" colours from any picture—allowing for designs with vector artwork and pictures using shared colours. Colours can be added to (or replace) your current document palette.

- **Automatic gradient fill swatches** (see p. 116)
  DrawPlus additionally offers gradient fill swatches which are not fixed to specific colours. Instead, an object's solid fill or its current Start/End fill path colours are used.

- **Vintage "Hands On" Phenakistoscopes** (see p. 36)
  The **Phenakistoscope QuickShape** is perfect for creating the illusion of motion—using a cut out of your designed and printed phenakistoscope, a pencil and a mirror!

Ease of Use

- **Non-printing background page colours** (see p. 14)
  Apply a background colour to your page(s) or spread that doesn't show on export or print.

- **Advanced photo editing with PhotoPlus** (see DrawPlus Help)
  Easily open any selected picture in Serif PhotoPlus or other photo-editing program of your choice. On saving, changes to your picture appear automatically back in DrawPlus.

Professional

- **Simpler PDF publishing** (see p. 189)
  A new and improved dialog offers only commonly used PDF settings via selectable profiles; advanced settings are stored under a collapsed More Options section if needed. PDF/X-3 compatibility is now provided via profile.

- **PDF Preview** (see p. 185)
  Interactive Print Preview now allows for **PDF publishing**, with all the benefits of preview—imposition at publish time, scaling, page mark control, view controls, and of course a screen-wide representation of your intended PDF output.

- **New PANTONE PLUS SERIES** (see DrawPlus Help)
  To add to DrawPlus's already extensive PANTONE libraries, the **PANTONE PLUS SERIES** is now included, which is, in turn, complemented by the **PANTONE Goe™ System**.

Animation

- **Joints for natural movement** (see p. 176)
  Both Keyframe and Stopframe animation now benefit from joint-based locking and rotating. Animated characters spring to life with even more realistic motion—great for animating skeletons, puppets, dolls, cranes, diggers, and more.

Installation

Installing DrawPlus follows different procedures depending on whether you are installing from disc or via download.

> 💡 You can install your new version alongside previous versions and use them independently.
>
> 💡 32 or 64-bit DrawPlus X6 installs to respective 32 or 64-bit computers.

Installation procedure (from disc)

- Insert your purchased disc into your disc drive.

  - If AutoPlay is enabled on the drive, this automatically starts the Setup Wizard. Follow the on-screen instructions for install.
    -or-
  - If AutoPlay is not enabled (or doesn't start the install automatically), navigate to your program disc and double-click **autorun.exe**.

Installation procedure (from download)

- From serif.com, when logged into your Serif account, follow the on-screen instructions to download.

System Requirements

Minimum:

- Windows-based PC with DVD drive and mouse
- Operating systems:
  Microsoft Windows® XP SP3 (32 bit)
  Windows® Vista (32 or 64 bit)
  Windows® 7 (32 or 64 bit)
  Windows® 8 (32 or 64 bit)
- 512MB RAM (1GB RAM for 64-bit operation)
- 778MB free hard disk space
- 1024 x 768 monitor resolution

Additional disk resources and memory are required when editing large or complex documents.

> 📌 To enjoy the full benefit of brushes and their textures, you must be using a computer whose processor supports SSE (most modern computers do). On brush selection, an on-screen message will indicate if your computer is non-SSE.

Recommended:

As above but:

- Dual-processor PC technology

Optional:

- Windows-compatible printer
- TWAIN-compatible scanner and/or digital camera
- Pressure-sensitive pen tablet
- Internet account and connection required for accessing online resources

2 Getting Started

Getting Started **11**

Startup Wizard

Once DrawPlus has been installed, you're ready to start.

- For Windows Vista/7: Setup adds a **Serif DrawPlus X6** item to the **All Programs** submenu of the Windows **Start** menu. Use the Windows **Start** button to pop up the Start Menu, click on **All Programs** and then click the DrawPlus icon (or if DrawPlus is already running, choose **New>New from Startup Wizard** from the **File** menu).

- For Windows 8: The Setup routine during install adds a **Serif DrawPlus X6** entry to the desktop. Use the Windows **Start** button to pop up the desktop, and then click the DrawPlus icon.

On program launch, the Startup Wizard is displayed which offers different routes into DrawPlus:

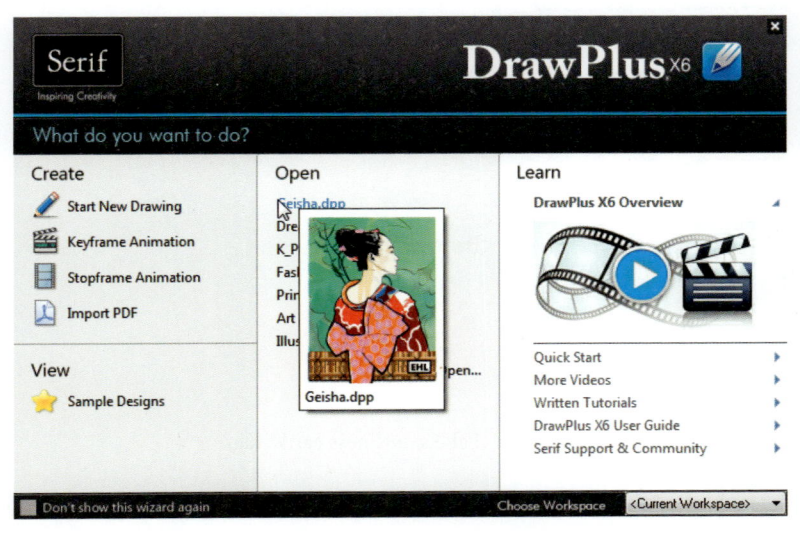

The Create and Open sections are self-explanatory, while the Learn section offers tutorials, the user guide, and other resources.

Starting with a new drawing

The first time you launch DrawPlus, you'll see the **Startup Wizard**, with a menu of choices. The **Start New Drawing** option offers an easy way to create your new drawing and lets you choose the initial setup for the particular type of document you'll be producing.

During **Page Setup**, DrawPlus offers a wide range of preset document types from several categories:

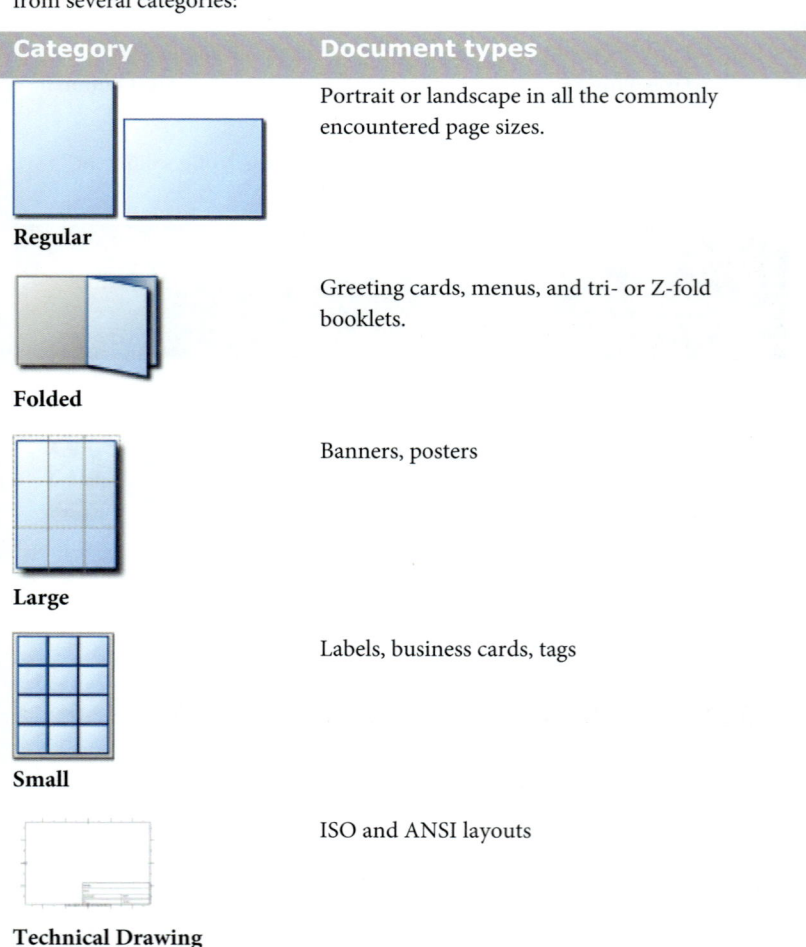

Category	Document types
Regular	Portrait or landscape in all the commonly encountered page sizes.
Folded	Greeting cards, menus, and tri- or Z-fold booklets.
Large	Banners, posters
Small	Labels, business cards, tags
Technical Drawing	ISO and ANSI layouts

To start a new drawing from scratch using the Startup Wizard:

1. Start DrawPlus (or choose **File>New>New from Startup Wizard** if it's already running).

2. Select **Start New Drawing** from the Startup Wizard.

3. From **Page Setup**, review document categories in the left-hand pane (and sub-categories if applicable). Categories contain preset document types (see above) or if you select **Regular**, you can choose from standard document sizes presented in Portrait or Landscape sub-categories.

4. Select a document type thumbnail from a category in the left-hand pane.

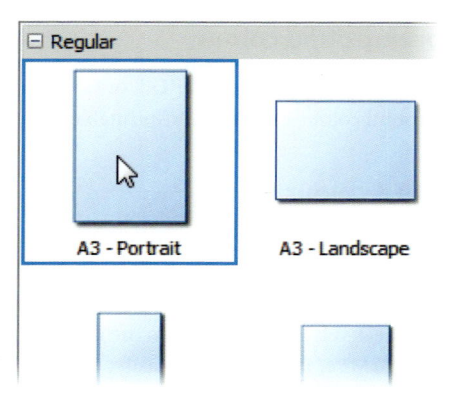

5. (Optional) For custom settings, on the right-hand pane, click a **Paper**, **Folding**, or **Margins** setting—choose a different drop-down list option or input new values to modify. Typically, you can change paper Width, Height, and Orientation settings in the **Paper** category.

6. (Optional) Set your colour mode to either RGB or CMYK from the **Primary Colour Mode** section. CMYK is used for professional printing. For more details, see Working in RGB or CMYK colour mode.

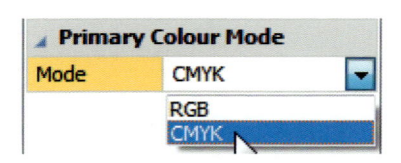

7. Click **OK**. The new document opens.

14 Getting Started

To start a new drawing during your DrawPlus session:

- Click **New Drawing** on the **Standard** toolbar (if Startup Wizard is disabled).

  - or -

  Choose **New>New Drawing** from the **File** menu.

> You can always adjust the page settings later via **File>Page Setup**.

> To start with a new keyframe or stopframe animation, see Getting started with animation on p. 165.

Changing the page background colour

The page background can be coloured with any HSL, RGB, or CMYK colour while you design. The background colour is always non-printable.

Working in RGB or CMYK colour mode

Whichever document type you choose, you'll be able to begin your design in either RGB or CMYK colour modes. The former is suitable when creating graphics for the web; the latter is ideal for professional pre-press PDF or image output (see p. 190 or p. 192, respectively). At any point in the future, you can change from RGB to CMYK, or CMYK to RGB modes easily.

> You can check which colour mode you are operating in, by viewing the Title Bar.

Opening a drawing

You can open an existing DrawPlus drawing from the Startup Wizard, **Standard** toolbar or the **File** menu.

To open an existing document from the Startup Wizard:

1. From the Startup Wizard (at startup time or via **File>New>New From Startup Wizard**), review your drawings in the **Open** section. The most recently opened file will be shown at the top of the list. To see a thumbnail preview of any file before opening, hover over its name in the list.

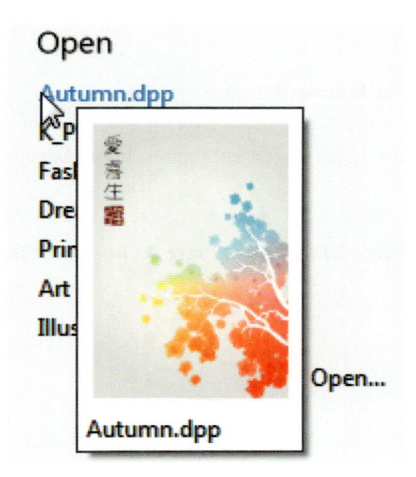

2. Click the file name to open it.

> If your drawing hasn't been opened recently, click **Open** to navigate to it.

To open an existing document via toolbar or menu:

1. Click **Open** on the **Standard** toolbar, or select **File>Open**.

2. In the Open dialog, navigate to, then select the file name and click the **Open** button.

> You can also open a range of file types including images, PDF documents, and Adobe Illustrator files.

Once a drawing is opened in its own document window, the window (and drawing) can be made currently active from a Document tab (below) or via the **Window** menu.

Saving your work

DrawPlus saves its documents as .dpp (Drawing) , .dpx (Template) or .dpa (Animation) files (for Stopframe and Keyframe animation modes).

To save your work:

- Click **Save** on the **Standard** toolbar.

    - or -

    To save the document under its current name, choose **Save** from the **File** menu.

    - or -

    To save under a different name, choose **Save As** from the **File** menu.

3 Pages

Using the page and pasteboard

Most of the DrawPlus display is taken up by a **page** or "artwork" area and a surrounding **pasteboard** area. This arrangement is an electronic equivalent of the system used by traditional graphic designers.

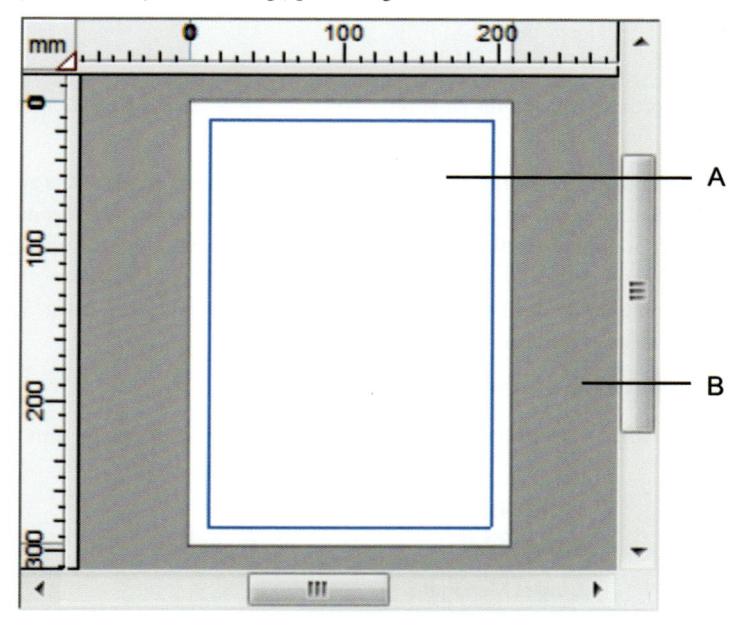

(A) Page and (B) Pasteboard

The **page area** is where you put the text and graphic elements that you want to be part of the final output. The **pasteboard area** is where you generally keep any elements that are being prepared or waiting to be positioned on the page area.

Setting measurement units and drawing scale

For precision drawing, you need techniques that allow you to position and draw accurately without effort, that will also be of use at any scaled size. Such techniques make use of rulers and guides for actual-size or scaled drawings.

Rulers

The rulers that surround the page allow you to measure the exact position of an object.

Ruler units used by DrawPlus determine the units displayed on the rulers and the reported units shown when positioning and scaling objects (either around the object or on the **Hintline**). You can change the ruler units without altering the document's dimensions. Unit settings are saved with your DrawPlus drawing; as a result loading different drawings, templates, etc. may change your working measurement units.

To change the measurement unit:

- Right-click on a ruler and select an alternative measurement unit.

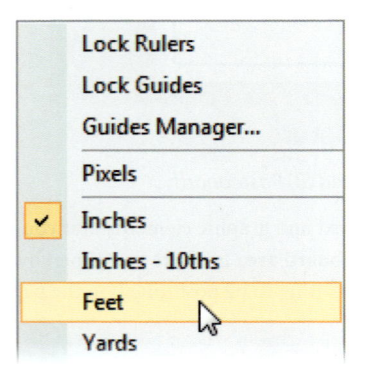

> Ruler Units are equivalent to Page Unit unless you're working on a scale drawing. For example, one ruler centimetre equals one centimetre on the printed page.

Creating guides

If you want to position objects repeatedly on the same horizontal or vertical boundary then **guides** can be used. DrawPlus lets you set up horizontal and vertical **guides**—non-printing, red lines you can use to align one object with another.

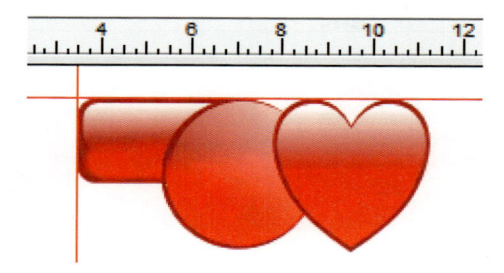

Guides can be created (and positioned) either by dragging from a ruler or via the **Guides Manager** (right-click any ruler). Both methods let you add guides to the current page, or, if creating a folded document, guides across a page spread.

To show/hide guides:

- To **show** or **hide** guides, check or uncheck **Layout Tools>Guides** from the **View** menu.

Drawing scale

You can create **scale drawings** (such as a home/garden design or model diagram) by setting a ratio other than 1:1 between page units and ruler units. For example, you might wish to set one page centimetre equivalent to 0.5 metre, a good scaling ratio for designing gardens of a typical size.

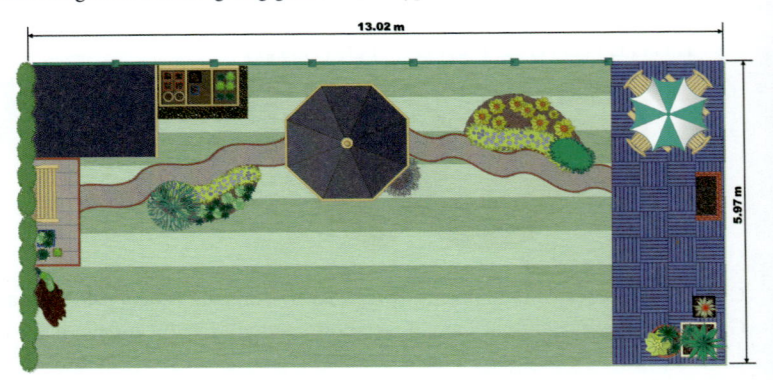

💡 Use Dimension tools (see p. 54) in conjunction with scale drawings for on-the-page measurements, which automatically update as you move objects.

To change the drawing scale:

1. Choose **Drawing Scale Options** from the context toolbar (shown with Pointer or Rotate Tool selected).
   Choose

2. Check the **Scale Drawing** box.

3. Use the input boxes to set the drawing scale as a proportion between the Page Distance (in **page units** that define the document's actual printing dimensions) and the Ruler Distance (in on-screen **ruler units** that represent the "real world" objects you're depicting).

Viewing pages

Once you've got a page in view, you can use the scrollbars at the right and bottom of the main window to move the page and pasteboard with respect to the main window. As you drag objects to the edge of the screen the scroll bars adjust automatically as the object is kept in view.

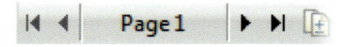

The Hintline toolbar at the bottom of the screen displays the current page number and provides a number of controls to let you navigate around your pages.

As an alternative, the Pages tab shows your pages as thumbnails, which when selected, will display that page in your workspace.

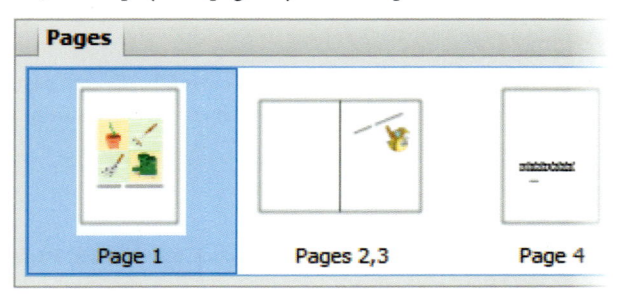

To navigate pages:

- Click **Previous page**, **Next page**, **First page** or **Last page** on the HintLine toolbar.

To go to a specific page:

1. Display the **Pages tab** (docked at the bottom of your DrawPlus workspace) by clicking the button.

2. Click on a thumbnail to jump directly to that page.

> For folded documents such as greeting cards, the "inner" page spread will show as "Pages 2,3". When the thumbnail is selected, the page spread is shown in your workspace.

Zooming

The **Hintline** toolbar also allows the user to view and/or edit the page at different levels of detail. You can use the **Zoom Tool**, **Pan Tool**, **Current Zoom**, **Zoom Out/In** (with slider), and **Fit Page** options.

If you're using a wheel mouse, you can scroll the wheel forward or back to move up or down the page. Try combining the **Ctrl** key and scrolling up or down for immediate in/out zoom control.

Adding and deleting pages

DrawPlus lets you add a page after the last page in your drawing.

You can also add one or more pages before or after a currently selected page; you can even make use of an object "cloning" feature which copies objects from a chosen page.

To add a new page:

- From the last page of the current drawing, click the ▶ **Next Page** button on the Hintline toolbar.

> The document format (as determined in **File>Page Setup**) will determine whether or not you can add or delete pages. For example, Folded documents have a fixed number of pages.

To delete one or more pages:

1. On Page Manager's **Delete Page** tab, specify the following:
   - The number of pages to delete
   - The page after which pages should be deleted
2. Click **OK**.

4 Lines, Curves, and Shapes

Lines, Curves, and Shapes **27**

Selecting one or more objects

Before you can change any object, you need to select it using one of several tools available from the top of the **Drawing** toolbar.

Pointer Tool/Rotate Tool
From the Selection tool flyout, click the **Pointer Tool** to select, move, copy, resize, or rotate objects. Use the **Rotate Tool** to exclusively select and rotate an object around a centre of rotation. You can also use the Rotate Tool to move or copy objects.

Node Tool
Click to use the **Node Tool** to manipulate the shape of objects, or move or copy objects.

To select an object:

- Click on the object using one of the tools shown above. For the Pointer and Rotate Tools, small "handles" appear around the object indicating selection.

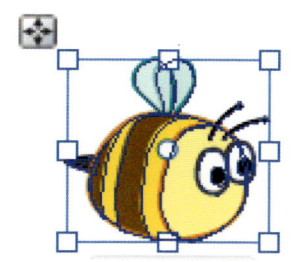

For the Node Tool, editable nodes are displayed for lines—sliding handles are additionally shown for adjustment of QuickShapes and text. If objects overlap, use the **Alt** key while clicking repeatedly until the desired item is selected.

> If an object won't select, it may be on another layer. Try clicking **Edit All Layers** on the **Layers** tab to allow selections to be made on any layer.

28 *Lines, Curves, and Shapes*

Selecting multiple objects

It is also possible to select more than one object, making a **multiple selection** that you can manipulate as if it were one object, or turn into a grouped object (p. 93).

To select more than one object (multiple selection):

1. Choose the **Pointer Tool** or **Rotate Tool**.

2. Click in a blank area of the page and drag a "marquee" box around the objects you want to select.

Release the mouse button. All of the objects within the marquee box are selected and one selection box, with handles, appears around the objects. To deselect, click in a blank area of the page.

- or -

1. Click on the first object for selection.

2. Press the **Shift** key down then click on a second object.

3. Continue selecting other objects to build up your multiple selection. Handles (or a bounding box, depending on the tool) appear around the multiple selection.

To select all objects on the page:

- Choose **Select All** from the **Edit** menu (or use **Ctrl+A**).

To add or remove an object from a multiple selection:

- Hold down the **Shift** key and click the object to be added or removed.

If you have one or more objects selected, you can select all other unselected page objects instead; the originally selected objects become deselected.

To invert a selection:

- From the **Edit** menu, select **Invert Selection**.

> For very precise object selection, you can draw a lasso around an object to select it (press the **Alt** Key down with the selection tool enabled, then drag around the object).

Drawing lines and shapes

Lines can be either straight or curved, and can have properties like **colour** and **width** (thickness). They can also adopt specific **line styles**, **ends**, and **caps**.

If you're using a pen tablet or using simulated pressure sensitivity (with DrawPlus's Pressure tab), you'll be able to draw realistic lines of varying width and opacity using pressure sensitivity—just like drawing with real pencils and pens.

Drawing lines

To draw a freeform line:

1. Choose the **Pencil Tool** from the **Drawing** toolbar.
2. Click once, then drag across the page, drawing a line as you go. The line appears immediately and follows your mouse movements.
3. To end the line, release the mouse button. The line will automatically smooth out using a minimal number of nodes. Note the little squares indicating its nodes—at the two ends, and at each point where two line segments come together.

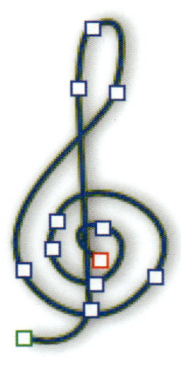

4. (Optional) To set the degree of smoothing to be applied to the line (and subsequent lines), set the **Smoothness** value on the context toolbar above your workspace.

To draw a straight line:

1. From the **Drawing** toolbar's Line Tools flyout, click the **Straight Line Tool**.

2. Click where you want the line to start, and drag to another point while holding down the mouse button, then release the mouse button. The straight line appears immediately.

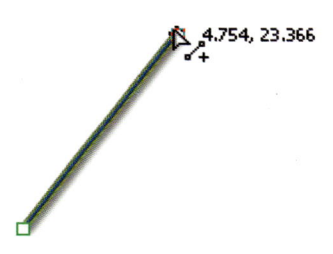

Any kind of open line (that is, one that hasn't been closed to create a shape) can be extended, and you can use any of the three line tools to do so.

To extend a line:

1. Move the cursor over either of the end nodes, a small cursor will appear. Click at that location.

2. The line that you drag out will be a continuation of the existing line, as a new line segment.

To draw a curved line:

1. Choose the **Pen Tool** from the **Drawing** toolbar's Pen Tools flyout.

2. From the displayed context toolbar, choose to create your drawn segments in **Smooth**, **Smart**, or **Line Segments** creation **Mode**.

- **Smooth Segments**: draws Bézier curves smoothly segment-by-segment, with manual on-curve and off-curve adjustment via nodes and control handles, respectively.

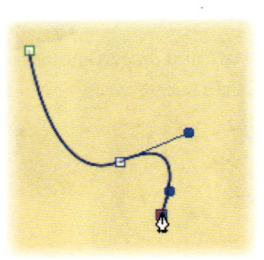

- **Smart Segments** (default): automatically determines slope and depth for a rounded, best-fitting curve. No control handle adjustment is normally necessary.

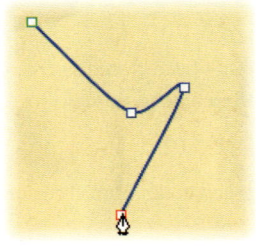

- **Line Segments**: creates a zig-zag line without curving through nodes.

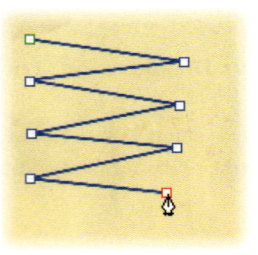

See DrawPlus Help for an in-depth look at drawing lines in each of these modes.

Drawing shapes

When a line (or series of line segments) forms a complete, enclosed outline, it becomes a new **closed** object called a **shape**. Because shapes have an interior region that can be filled (for example, with a solid colour or a bitmap), they have fill properties as well as line properties.

You can make a shape by closing a curve—extending a freeform line or a segmented straight line back to its starting point. Shapes have an interior which is filled with the current **default fill** (see Setting fill properties on p. 103) when the shape is closed.

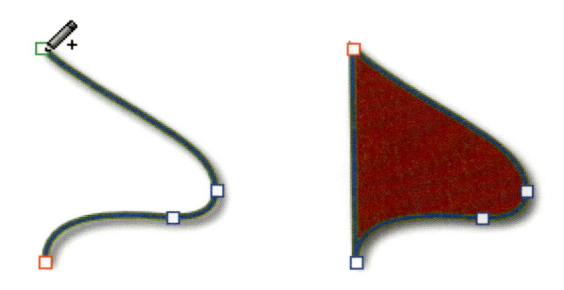

To close an existing curve (with a straight line):

1. Select the curve with the **Node Tool**, **Pencil** or **Pen Tool**.

2. Click **Close Curve** on the context toolbar. A Straight segment appears, closing the curve.

To close a curve (without new segment):

- Select the curve with the **Node Tool**, and drag from an end node (note the Node cursor), moving the line, onto the other end node (a Close cursor will show); releasing the mouse button will create a shape.

If you're trying to draw an outline made up of many independent curves (e.g., a cartoon ear, rose, etc.) and you want to retain the fill colour, you can fill each curve without closing them. This is made easy by using the **Fill-on-Create** feature.

To fill an unclosed curve automatically:

1. Select the Pencil Tool, Pen Tool, or Brush Tool.

2. Enable **Fill-on-Create** from the context toolbar, and select a suitable fill from the Colour tab. You'll also need to ensure **Select-on-Create** is enabled on the context toolbar (Freehand and Brush tools only).

3. Draw a freeform line, pen line, or brush stroke into a curve. The resulting curve is filled with the current fill colour.

Using QuickShapes

QuickShapes are pre-designed objects that you can instantly add to your page, then adjust and morph into a variety of further QuickShapes. QuickShapes are added from a flyout containing a wide variety of commonly used shapes, including boxes, arrows, hearts, spirals and other useful symbols.

Morphing to new shapes can be carried out after you add the QuickShape to the page (or as you add by double-clicking on the page).

To create a QuickShape:

1. Click the down arrow on the **QuickShape** button on the **Drawing** toolbar, then select a shape from the flyout.

   The button takes on the icon of the shape you selected.

2. At your chosen cursor position, click and drag on the page to draw out your QuickShape to a chosen size (use the **Shift** key to lock the aspect ratio; the **Ctrl** key to scale from its centre point; or both together).

New QuickShapes adopt the currently set line and fill in DrawPlus.

> **Ctrl**-double-click to place a default-sized QuickShape on the page.

36 *Lines, Curves, and Shapes*

To adjust the appearance of a QuickShape:

1. With the **Node Tool** (**Drawing** toolbar) selected, click on the QuickShape to reveal sliding handles around the shape. These are distinct from the "inner" selection handles. Different QuickShapes have different handles.

2. Drag any handle to change the appearance of the QuickShape.

For example, by dragging the top sliding handle to the right on the pentagon below will quickly produce an octagon:

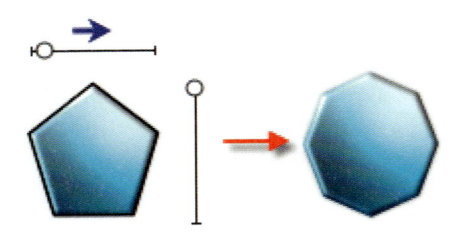

One particular QuickShape, called Quick Phenakistoscope, is based on the magic lantern effect, and can be used to create the illusion of movement by spinning the printed phenakistoscope in a mirror, while looking through a one of the cutout slits.

Lines, Curves, and Shapes **37**

Drawing spirals

By their nature, spirals are very difficult to draw accurately. In DrawPlus, a dedicated Spiral Tool is available to make life a little easier. Some interesting designs are possible with a little experimentation.

To draw a spiral:

1. From the **Drawing** toolbar's Pen Tools flyout, click the **Spiral Tool**.

2. Click where you want the spiral to originate from, then drag out to size your spiral.

38 Lines, Curves, and Shapes

3. (Optional) As you drag, several shortcuts can be used to modify the spiral as you draw:

   Press the **X** key to flip the spiral (change its direction). Press again to flip back.

   Use the left/right arrow key to increase/decrease the spiral spacing, i.e. the number of line segments that make up the spiral.

   Use the down arrow key to decrease the spiral length from its origin; the up arrow does the opposite.

4. Release the mouse button to complete your spiral.

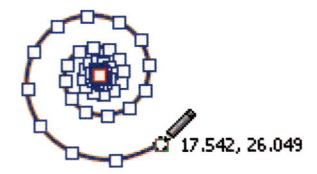

5. Click away from the spiral to complete your spiral.

For more information about modifying your spiral, see Editing lines and shapes on p. 43.

As your spiral is basically a line made up of curved line segments, you can also apply line properties (p. 109) to it.

Lines, Curves, and Shapes **39**

Drawing arcs

The **Arc Tool** provides a convenient way of creating smooth arcs without the need to worry about adjusting nodes and curve control handles. In addition, modifier keys are on hand so you can quickly adapt your arc as you draw, providing many design possibilities.

To draw an arc:

1. From the **Drawing** toolbar's Line Tools flyout, click the **Arc Tool**.

2. Click where you want the arc to originate then drag out to draw it on the page.

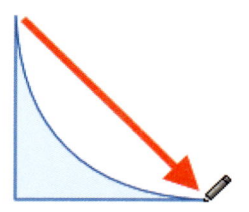

By default, the arc is drawn as a **concave, closed shape**.

3. (Optional) As you drag, several modifier keys can be used to adjust the arc:

    - Press the **C** key to draw an arc as a single **line**. Press again to revert to a closed shape.

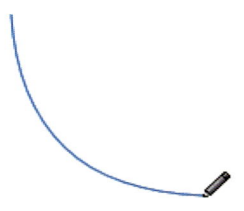

    - Press the **X** key to change the direction of the arc to **convex**. Press again to revert to a concave arc.

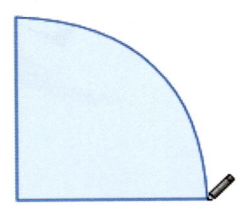

    - Use the **up/down arrow** keys to adjust the **depth** of the arc as you draw.

4. Release the mouse button to complete the arc.

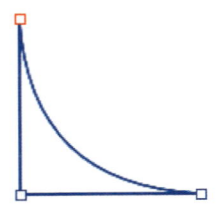

Modifying arcs

Once drawn, your arc becomes a closed shape or single line composed of nodes and curve control handles. This means you can modify your arc in the same way you would edit any other shapes and lines. See Editing lines and shapes on p. 43 for more information.

Furthermore, you can apply generic line properties (p. 109) to your arc.

If you used the **C** key to modify your arc into a single line, you can extend the line using the **Pencil Tool**, **Pen Tool**, **Straight Line Tool** and, of course, the **Arc Tool**.

Drawing triangles

The **Triangle Tool** provides a convenient way of drawing triangles of varying shapes and sizes.

To draw a triangle:

1. From the **Drawing** toolbar's Line Tools flyout, click the **Triangle Tool**.

2. Click and drag out to draw a triangle on the page.

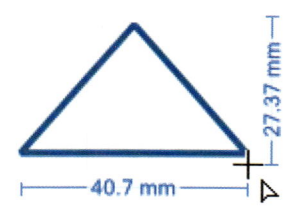

3. (Optional) As you drag, several modifier keys can be used to adjust the triangle:

- Hold down the **Ctrl** key to draw the triangle from a central point.

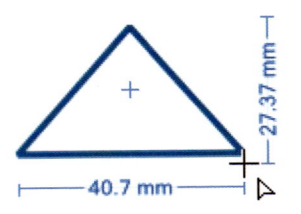

- Hold down the **Shift** key to constrain the shape to an equilateral triangle.

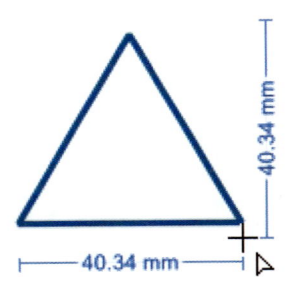

4. Release the mouse button to complete the triangle.

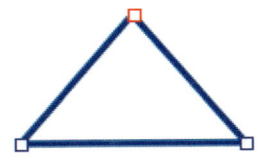

Modifying triangles

Your drawn triangle is composed of nodes and curve control handles and can be adjusted in the same way you would edit any other shape. The **Triangle Tool** automatically switches to the **Node Tool** when the drawing has been completed to aid in modifying your triangle.

To modify a triangle:

- With the triangle and **Node Tool** selected, click and drag any node or line to modify the shape.

Furthermore, you can apply generic line properties (p. 109) to your triangle.

Editing lines and shapes

To edit lines or shapes, you can manipulate their segments, on-curve nodes, and off-curve control handles allowing you to:

- Redraw part of a line
- Reshape a line
- Simplify a line (remove nodes)
- Enhance a line (add nodes)
- Change the type of node or line segment

> ★ The procedures relate to lines drawn with the Pencil Tool, but also to curves drawn with the Pen Tool. For simplicity, we'll only use the term line.

44   *Lines, Curves, and Shapes*

Redrawing part of a line

With the **Pencil Tool**, it's easy to redraw any portion of a line.

To redraw part of a selected line:

1. Select the line, then the **Pencil Tool**. Hover the displayed cursor on the line where you want to begin redrawing. The cursor changes to indicate you can begin drawing.

2. Click on the line, and a new node appears.

3. Keep the mouse button down and drag to draw a new line section, connecting it back to another point on the original line. Again, the cursor changes to include a curve when you're close enough to the line to make a connection. When you release the mouse button, the original portion is replaced by the newly drawn portion.

Lines, Curves, and Shapes **45**

Reshaping a line

The main tool for editing lines and shapes is the **Node Tool**. You can drag segments or select one or more nodes on the object, then use the buttons on the tool's supporting context toolbar to adjust.

To reshape a curved line:

1. Click the **Node Tool** on the **Drawing** toolbar.
2. Select any line on your page. The line's on-curve nodes appear, and the context toolbar also pops up.
3. Hover over a segment and drag the segment to form a new curve shape.

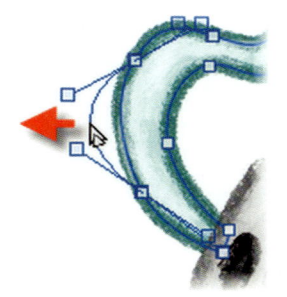

-or-

Select nodes and drag. Selection can be by one of the following methods:

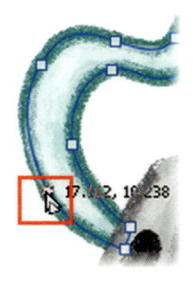

Hover over a single node and click to select the node. ***Shift****-click for multiple nodes.*

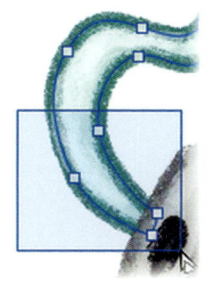

Drag out a marquee to select multiple neighbouring nodes

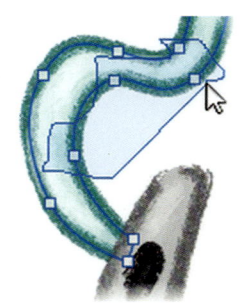

*Drag out a lasso (with **Alt** key pressed) to select multiple nodes otherwise difficult to select via a marquee.*

46 Lines, Curves, and Shapes

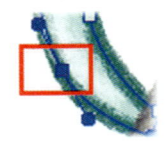

Once a square **end node** or **interior node** is selected, the node becomes highlighted and off-curve rounded **control handles** for all line segment(s) will appear. A single control handle shows on an end node; a pair of handles will show on a selected interior node.

Remember that a segment is the line between two nodes; each node provides two control handles, with each handle controlling different adjoining segments. One control handle in a segment works in conjunction with the control handle on the opposite end of the segment.

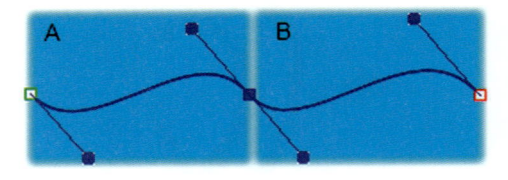

*(**A**) Line Segment 1, (**B**) Line Segment 2*

4. Drag any selected node to reshape adjacent segment(s).
5. Drag one or more control handles to produce very precise changes in the curvature of the line on either side of a node. You can shorten or lengthen the handles, which changes the depth of the **curve** (that is, how far out the curve extends), or alter the handle angle, which changes the curve's **slope**.

Simplifying or enhancing a line

The more nodes there are on a line or shape, the more control over its shape you have. The fewer nodes there are, the simpler (smoother) the line or shape.

To adjust the smoothness of the most recent pencil line:

1. Choose the **Pencil Tool** and draw a freeform line.
2. From the context toolbar, click the right arrow on the **Smoothness** option and drag the displayed slider left to increase the number of nodes.
3. To make the curve less complex, i.e. smoother, drag the slider right to decrease the number of nodes.

To add or delete a node:

- To **add a node**, click along a line segment with the Node Tool or Pen Tool to add a new node at that point. The new node will be created and will be selected.

- To **delete a node**, select the line with the Node Tool then the node itself and click the **Delete Node** button on the context toolbar (or press the **Delete** key). The node will be deleted, and the line or shape will jump to its new shape. With the Pen Tool selected, you can also delete a node by clicking on it.

You can also use the Node Tool to reposition the nodes, and reshape the line or shape, by dragging on the new handles.

Changing nodes and line segments

Each segment in a line has a control handle at either end, so at each interior or "corner" node (where two segments join) you'll see a pair of handles. The behaviour of these handles—and thus the curvature of the segments to either side—depends on whether the node is set to be **sharp**, **smooth**, **symmetric**, or **smart**. You can quickly identify a node's type by selecting it and seeing which button is selected in the displayed context toolbar. Each type's control handles behave differently as described below.

To change one or more nodes to a different type:

1. Select the object with the **Node Tool**, followed by the node(s) you want to change.

2. Click one of the node buttons on the displayed context toolbar.

A **Sharp Corner** means that the line segments to either side of the node are completely independent so that the corner can be quite pointed.

A **Smooth Corner** uses Bézier curves, which means that the slope of the line is the same on both sides of the node, but the depth of the two joined segments can be different.

At a **Symmetric Corner**, nodes join line segments with the same slope and depth on both sides of the node.

Smart Corner nodes automatically determine slope and depth for a rounded, best-fitting curve. If you attempt to adjust a smart corner's handles, it becomes a smooth corner. You can always reset the node to smart—but to maintain smart nodes, be careful what you click on!

Converting a shape to editable curves

The conversion of QuickShapes to curves provides you with a starting point for your own shapes (below), whereas converting text to curves is one way of incorporating editable letter-based shapes into designs.

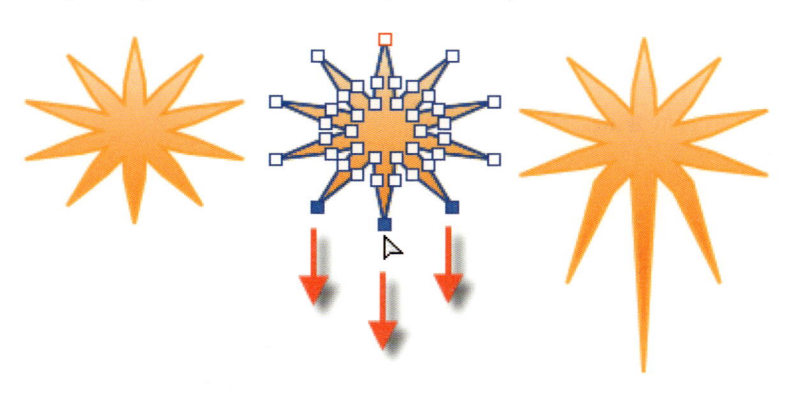

To convert an object into curves:

1. Select your QuickShape or text object.

2. Click **Convert to Curves** on the Arrange tab.

3. With the **Node Tool** enabled (Drawing toolbar), edit the curve outline by dragging selected nodes.

> The conversion process loses all of the special properties inherent in QuickShapes and text.

Connectors

Connectors are special lines that you can anchor to objects, where they remain attached even if one or both objects are moved or resized. Using connectors, you can easily create dynamic diagrams and charts that show relationships, such as family trees, organization charts, and flow charts. If you need to rearrange the elements, the connections are preserved.

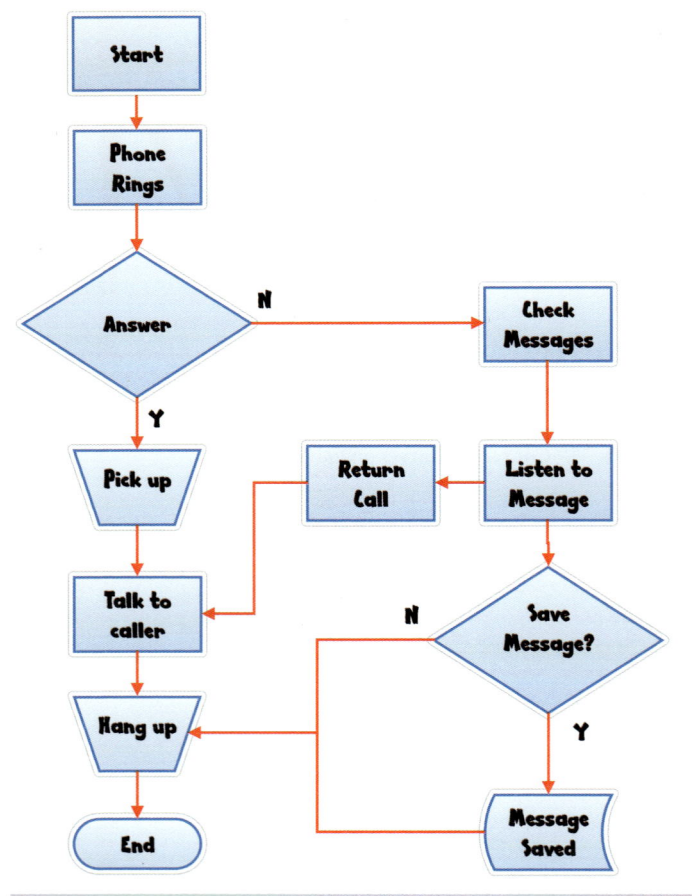

> 💡 Try the Gallery tab (Office folder) for flow chart (above), network, and organization chart symbols, then simply add connectors between objects.

Lines, Curves, and Shapes **51**

A key feature of connectors is that if you move any connected object at a later date, the connectors will follow.

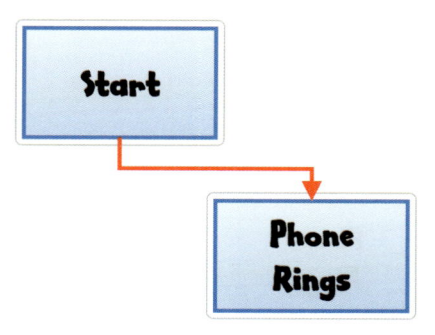

To create a connection:

1. Select **Connector Tool** on the Pen Tools flyout (**Drawing** toolbar). Hover over an object so that default connection points become visible.

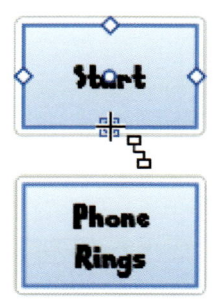

2. On the displayed context toolbar, ensure **Auto Connector Tool** is selected. This creates intelligent Auto Connectors.

52 Lines, Curves, and Shapes

3. Click the connection point on the object and drag to the destination object—you'll see potential "target" connection points display (in red) on the destination object.

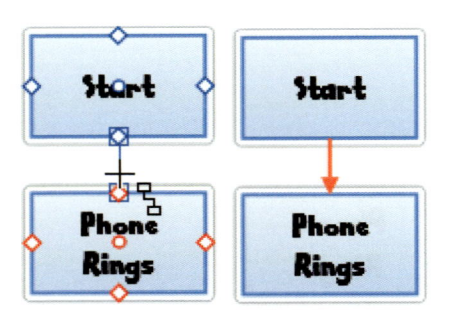

Once you've created a connector, DrawPlus lets you adjust the connector's path or edit the properties of a connector by dragging the connector line or nodes.

To edit the selected connector's properties (line colour, width, style, and end):

- Select options from the Connector context toolbar at the top of your workspace.

To branch connectors:

- Use **Ctrl+Alt**-drag to copy a connector and connected object simultaneously—great for creating branched connectors. Select the connected object only in advance.

Lines, Curves, and Shapes **53**

Connector types

We've used the Auto Connector Tool exclusively so far. However, this tool exists among a selection of connector tools, each designed for different uses. The **Connector Tool**, when selected, offers the different types of connector tool on the Connectors context toolbar situated above the workspace.

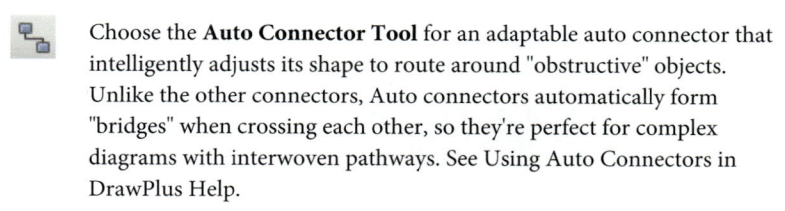

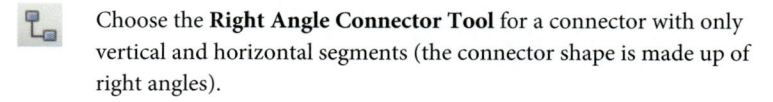

Choose the **Auto Connector Tool** for an adaptable auto connector that intelligently adjusts its shape to route around "obstructive" objects. Unlike the other connectors, Auto connectors automatically form "bridges" when crossing each other, so they're perfect for complex diagrams with interwoven pathways. See Using Auto Connectors in DrawPlus Help.

Choose the **Direct Connector Tool** to draw a single, straight-line connector between any two connection points.

Choose the **Right Angle Connector Tool** for a connector with only vertical and horizontal segments (the connector shape is made up of right angles).

To change the connector type:

1. Select the connector with the Pointer Tool.

2. Select an Auto, Right Angle, Direct, or Custom connector type from the context toolbar.

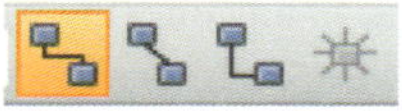

- or -

- Right-click the connector and choose equivalent options from the Connectors flyout.

Adding dimension lines and labels

DrawPlus lets you add **dimension lines** with text **labels** showing the distance between two fixed points in a drawing, or the angle formed by three points. For example, you can draw a dimension line along one side of a box, measuring the distance between the two corner points. If you resize the box, the line automatically follows suit, and its label text updates to reflect the new measurement.

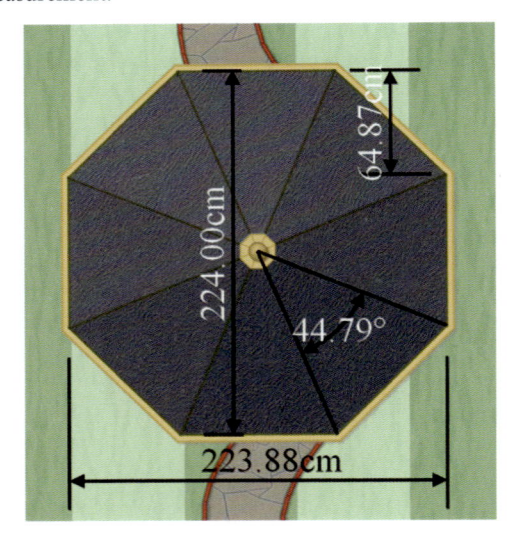

You'll find dimension lines indispensable for planning garden designs (e.g., a garden gazebo plan), technical diagrams, floor plans, or any drawing where exact measurements and scale are important.

Although they can be drawn anywhere on the page, dimension lines are at their most accurate when attached to **connection points** on objects (see p. 53) or when snapped to **dynamic guides** (see DrawPlus Help).

To draw a dimension:

1. From the **Drawing** toolbar's Connector Tool flyout, select the **Dimension Tool**. (The flyout shows the icon of the most recently selected tool.)

2. Either, for a **linear dimension**, click the respective tool from the Dimension context toolbar:

- ⊢⊣ **Auto Dimension Line Tool**.
  Use to draw vertical, horizontal, or diagonal dimension lines in any direction, with automatic placement of the editable dimension label adjacent to the line.

  Click where you want to start the dimension line (e.g., on a connection point), then drag and release the mouse button where you want to end the line (maybe on another connection point). The illustrations below show the result of dragging between connection points on two Quick Squares with the Auto Dimension Line Tool enabled.

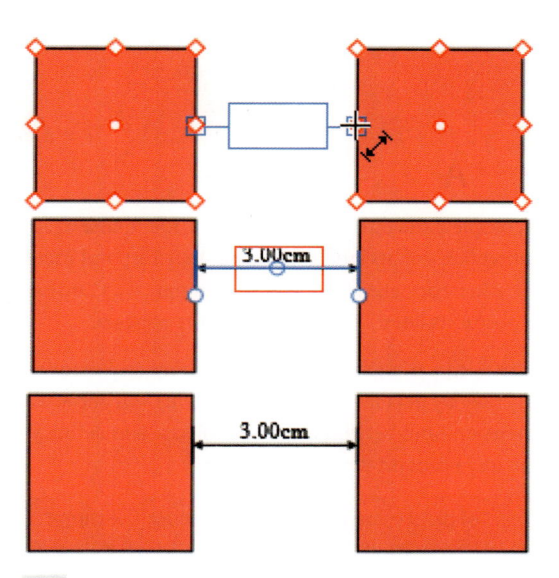

- **Vertical Dimension Line Tool**.
  Ideal for vertical dimension lines, the label information is always presented vertically with the option to move the label by dragging. Extension lines are used to present the dimension line vertically and to allow for an optional offset.

- **Horizontal Dimension Line Tool**.

   As above but for horizontal dimension lines.

- **Slanted Dimension Line Tool**.

   Designed specifically for drawing diagonal dimension lines.

- or -

For an **angular dimension**, click the **Angular Dimension Line Tool** then click and drag from a corner node towards the angle you want to measure (**A**). Release the mouse button over the "target" angle, then move your mouse cursor to the next corner node, then click on that node (**B**) to set the angle to be measured.

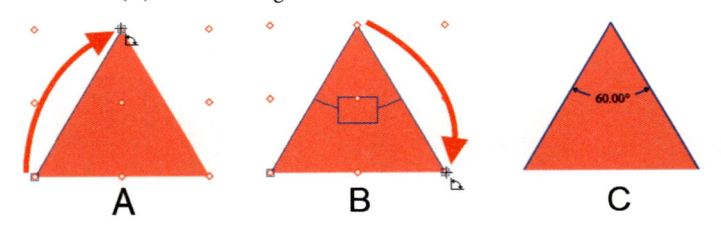

To complete the dimension line, move the mouse again to position the floating line and its label—note that they respond independently—and click when they are where you want them (**C**). (You can always change the positions later.) The dimension line appears.

We've used a triangle as an example above and made use of the nodes that show by default. However, DrawPlus will allow you to add dimension lines between separate objects, and define your target angle from any point on the object or page.

> Instead of displaying an inner angle, drag the dimension line and label to the outer angle to display its obtuse equivalent.

> Press the **Esc** key while drawing your dimension line to cancel the operation.

Adjusting dimension lines

For all dimension tools, a pair of parallel blue **extension lines** with blue end **nodes** appears on the dimension line, along with a node on the label box. Between the two extension lines, the dimension line and its label can "float" by moving the blue nodes.

Using the Gallery

The Studio's Gallery tab contains pre-built design objects and elements you'd like to reuse in different drawings. You can choose designs stored under Clipart (like Animals), Home, Office, School, ShapeArt, and Web folders.

The Gallery tab also lets you store your own designs in a **My Designs** section if you would like to reuse them—the design is made available in any DrawPlus drawing. You can add and delete your items within each category, with the option of naming elements to facilitate rapid retrieval.

> You can create your own folders and categories from the Gallery tab's ▷ **Tab Menu**.

To view your Gallery:

- Click the Studio's **Gallery** tab.
- Select a folder or category from the drop-down list. The items from the folder's first listed category are displayed by default.

To use a design from the Gallery:

- Drag any preset design directly onto the page. You can modify, then drag the design back into your own custom category.

To copy an object into the Gallery:

1. Display the Gallery tab's **My Designs** (or sub-category of that) where you want to store the object.

2. Drag the object from the page and drop it onto the gallery.

3. You'll be prompted to type a name for the design. (You can name or rename the design later, if you wish.) By default, designs are labelled as "Untitled."

4. A thumbnail of the design appears in the gallery, labelled with its name.

To delete or rename a custom design:

- Right-click its gallery thumbnail and choose **Delete Design** or **Rename Design** from the submenu.

5 Using Brushes

Selecting brushes

DrawPlus supports a wide range of brushes, all capable of producing:

Stroke brush effects:

- Draw (graphic pencil, marker pen, pen, pencil)
- Paint (bristle, stipple, wash)

Spray and photo brush effects:

- Airbrush, splats, spray can
- Effects (bubbles, glitter, neon, smoke, fur, clouds)
- Grunge
- Nature (fog, grass, snow)
- Photo (rope, chains, zippers, flowers, embroidery, textured edges)

Painting inherits the principles of Drawing lines and shapes (see p. 29). The drawing freedom of the Pencil Tool is adapted for brushwork using the dedicated **Brush Tool**. You can pick up colour for your brushes as you would for other object, by simply selecting the Brush Tool, choosing your **brush type** from the **Brushes tab** and picking a brush colour from context toolbar, Colour or Swatch tab.

Using Brushes

The Brushes tab lets you **select** a brush type from a range of categories. You can also view brushes currently being used in your document, and edit brushes (p. 65) or create your own brushes (see DrawPlus Help).

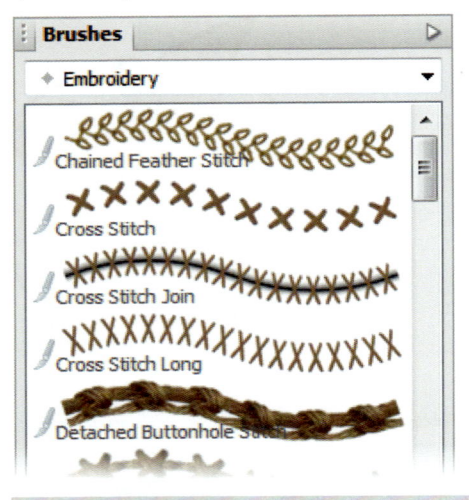

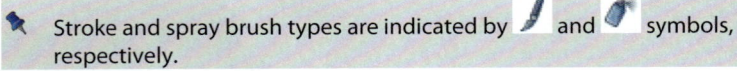

> Stroke and spray brush types are indicated by 🖌 and 🖌 symbols, respectively.

To make sense of all the brush types available to the user, the preset brushes are stored under a series of pre-defined categories under the name **Global**—the brushes are available to all DrawPlus documents currently open. The **Document** category shows the brush types currently in use in the DrawPlus drawing and is used to "bookmark" brushes for easy reuse in the future.

Applying brush strokes

The **Brush Tool** is used exclusively to apply brush strokes to the page. The tool is used in conjunction with the Brushes tab, and a supporting context toolbar.

To apply a brush stroke:

1. Select the **Brush Tool** from the **Drawing** toolbar.
2. Display the Brushes tab and choose a category from the drop-down list, then a brush.

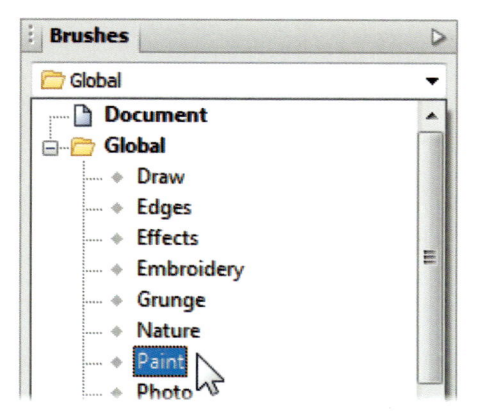

Bristle 01

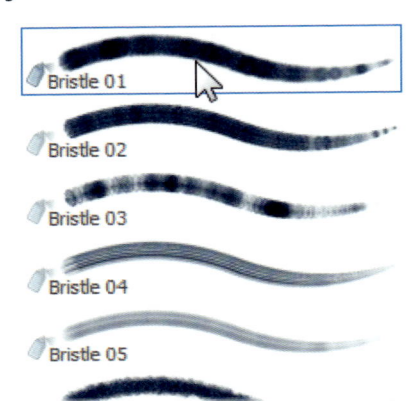

Bristle 02

Bristle 03

Bristle 04

Bristle 05

3. Select a **Line Colour**, **Width**, or **Opacity** from the context toolbar.

4. (Optional) For spray brushes, adjust **Flow** to control the density of paint laid down as you apply it, like "layering up" a brush then painting.

5. (Optional) From the context toolbar, adjust **Smoothness** (to set how smooth your stroke is applied).

6. (Optional) Enable **Select-on-Create** to leave the brush stroke selected on the page. If disabled, the stroke is left deselected.

7. (Optional) Enable **Fill-on-Create** to fill the unclosed curve produced by the brush stroke with the default fill colour.

8. With the brush cursor, drag across your page to create a brush stroke.

> Photo brushes, available from the Brushes tab (Photo category), can be recoloured just as any other brush type.

> You can also apply a brush stroke around an object's outline (shape, artistic text, picture, etc.) via **Brush Stroke** on the Line tab. See Setting line properties on p. 109.

Setting brush defaults

See Updating defaults in DrawPlus Help.

Editing brush strokes

It's possible to alter any previously drawn brush stroke with respect to its properties, brush type, and shape.

To change brush stroke properties:

- With the Brush Tool selected, use the context toolbar to adjust the properties of a brush stroke once it has been drawn on the page.

To change brush stroke type:

1. Select the brush stroke.
2. Go to the Brushes tab and select firstly a brush category, then a brush type from the displayed gallery. The brush stroke adopts the newly chosen brush.

> Brush types currently applied to your brush strokes are handily listed in the **Document** folder of the Brushes tab.

To change the shape of your brush stroke:

A brush stroke possesses very similar characteristics to a plain line. Any brush stroke can therefore be edited, extended, or redrawn with the **Node Tool** (**Drawing** toolbar) just as for a straight or curved line (see Editing lines and shapes on p. 43). Use for fine-tuning your brush strokes after application.

Pressure sensitivity

via a pen tablet

Your pen tablet and DrawPlus work in perfect harmony for a truly authentic drawing and painting experience, with in-built pressure sensitivity as you draw and paint. See DrawPlus Help for more information.

via the Pressure tab

If a pen tablet is unavailable to you, DrawPlus can simulate pressure sensitivity when using your mouse (along with DrawPlus's Pressure tab).

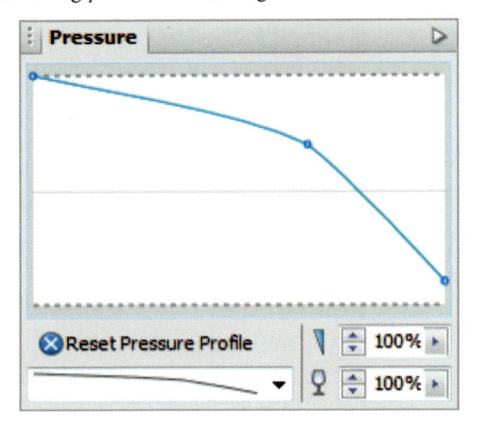

This tab is used to set pressure sensitivity globally by using a **pressure profile**.

To apply a pressure profile:

1. Expand the Pressure tab at the bottom right of your screen, and choose a pressure profile from the drop-down list.

    The pressure chart updates to reflect the chosen profile.

2. Apply a brush stroke or draw a line on the page. This will adopt the chosen pressure profile.

The profile is maintained until you reset it or pick another profile from the preset list. As well as using the preset profiles you can also create your own custom profile. (See DrawPlus Help for more details.)

6 Text

Entering text

You can create different types of text in DrawPlus, i.e. **Artistic Text**, **Frame Text**, or **Shape Text**, all directly on the page.

Artistic Text   *Frame Text*   *Shape Text*

It's easy to edit the text once it's created, by retyping it or altering properties like font, style, and point size.

In general, artistic text (as an independent object) is better suited to decorative or fancy typographic design, frame text is intended for presenting text passages in more traditional square or rectangular shaped blocks; shape text lends itself so well to blocks of body text where shape and flow contribute to the overall layout.

To enter new artistic text:

1. Select **A Artistic Text Tool** on the **Drawing** toolbar's Text flyout.

2. To create **artistic text** at the current default point size, click where you want to start the text.
   - or -
   For artistic text that will be automatically sized into an area, click and drag out the area to the desired size.

3. To set text attributes (font, size, etc.) before you start typing, make selections on the Text context toolbar. For colour, set the Line/Fill swatches on the Studio's Colour or Swatch tab.

4. Start typing.

To create frame text:

1. Select **Frame Text Tool** on the **Drawing** toolbar's Text flyout.

2. From the positioned cursor, either:

   - Double-click on the page to create a new frame at a default size.
     - or -
   - Drag out a frame to your desired frame dimension.

3. (Optional) Set text and colour attributes as for artistic text before you start typing.

4. Start typing within the frame.

To enter new shape text:

1. Create a QuickShape either from the **Drawing** toolbar's QuickShape flyout or by closing a drawn line.

2. With a shape still selected, select **Artistic Text** (**Drawing** toolbar) and just start typing.

For existing shapes without shape text, select the shape, then the **Artistic Text Tool**, then begin typing.

Editing text

Once you've entered either **artistic**, **frame** or **shape text** (see Entering text on p. 69), you can retype it and/or format its character attributes (font, point size, bold/italic/underline, subscript/superscript, OpenType font features, etc.), paragraph properties, and text flow. Text objects have graphic properties, too—artistic text behaves like an independent graphic object (it can be scaled), while shape or frame text conforms to its container or frame.

Artistic text, text frames, and shapes containing text can all be rotated, skewed, moved, and copied. You can also apply line and fill colour independently, brush strokes/edges, or apply opacity and transparency effects, for interesting text effects.

Colour can be applied to selected text as a solid, gradient or bitmap fill—for a solid fill, simply select one or more characters and apply a solid colour from the Studio's Colour tab (ensuring the fill swatch is set) or the Character dialog. See Setting fill properties on p. 103.

For a gradient or bitmap fill, use the Studio's Swatch tab. See p. 116 or p. 120, respectively.

Similarly, opacity is applied from the Colour tab (see p. 124); gradient and bitmap transparency from the Transparency tab.

Retyping text

You can either retype artistic, frame or shape text directly on the page, or use the Edit Text window—great for managing large amounts of text (overflowed shape text or otherwise) in a simple word processing environment.

To retype text on the page:

1. Select the object and then select **A Artistic Text** (from the **Drawing** toolbar's Text flyout) in either order.

2. Type new text at the selection point or drag to select text, then type to replace it. To cut, copy, and paste, use the toolbar buttons or standard Windows keyboard shortcuts.

To create a new line:

- At the position you want to start a new line, press the **Enter** key.

Formatting text

You can change text formatting (character, paragraph, bullets/numbering and text flow properties) directly on the page via the Text context toolbar or via a **Text Style** dialog.

To format selected text on the page:

1. Use the **Pointer Tool** to select the text you want to change.

   Alternatively, drag select on any text with **Artistic Text** (from the **Drawing** toolbar's Text flyout).

2. Use the Text context toolbar to change text properties (font, point size, bold/italic/underline, subscript/superscript, OpenType font features, text alignment, bullets and numbering, levels, and text fitting).

> For greater control over the shape of the artistic text characters, try converting the artistic text to **curves**. As curves, you can position every character individually and even edit the character shapes, exactly as if you had drawn the character shapes by hand using the line tools. For details, see Converting a shape to editable curves on p. 49.

Using fonts

If you plan to use text in your drawing, you can change the text's appearance dramatically by changing its font. In doing so, you can communicate very different messages to your target audience.

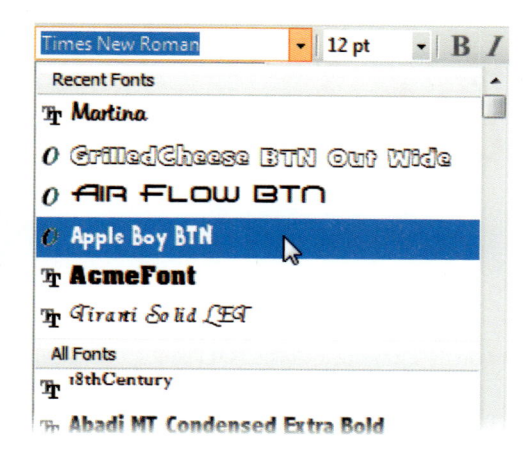

Font assignment is very simple in DrawPlus, and can be done from the Text context toolbar.

Fitting text to a path

DrawPlus allows you to make artistic text conform to a curved baseline (such as a drawn freeform line or curve), custom shape or a preset shape (QuickShape).

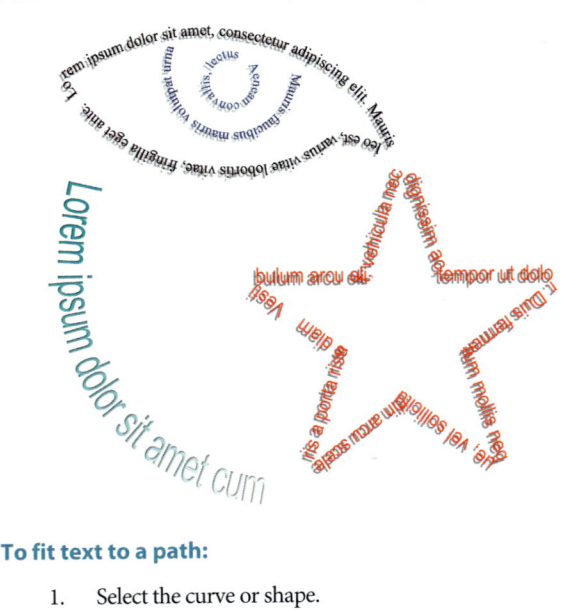

To fit text to a path:

1. Select the curve or shape.

2. Select **A** **Artistic Text** on the **Drawing** toolbar's Text flyout.

3. Hover over the curve or shape's outline until you see a cursor, then click at the point on the line where your text is to begin.

4. Begin typing your text. The text will be placed along the curve or shape.

To flow text along a preset path:

1. Select your artistic text.

2. From the context toolbar, click the down arrow on the **Preset Text Paths** button and select a preset curve from the drop-down list on which the text will flow.

7 Manipulating Objects

Copying, pasting, cutting, and deleting objects

To copy one or more objects to the Windows Clipboard:

1. Select the object(s).

2. Click the **Copy** button on the **Standard** toolbar.

If you're using another Windows application, you can usually copy and paste objects via the Clipboard.

To paste an object from the Clipboard:

- Click the **Paste** button on the **Standard** toolbar.

The standard Paste command inserts a clipboard object onto the page.

> To select the type of object to be pasted from the Clipboard, choose **Paste Special** from the **Edit** menu.

To cut one or more objects to the Clipboard:

1. Select the object(s).

2. Click the **Cut** button on the **Standard** toolbar.

The object is deleted from the page and a copy is placed on the Windows Clipboard.

To delete one or more objects:

- Select the object(s) with the **Pointer**, **Rotate** or **Node Tool** and press the **Delete** key.

Cloning an object

DrawPlus lets you "clone" or duplicate objects easily using drag-and-drop. A copy is displayed at the new location and the original object is still kept at the same position—your new copy also possesses the formatting of the original copied object.

Multiple copies of an individual object can also be made by replication or transformation.

Making duplicates

- Select the object, then press the **Ctrl** key.
- Drag the object via the ⊕ **Move** button to a new location on the page, then release the mouse button.

> Use duplication when rotating or shearing an object—the result is a new copy at a new angle, possibly overlapping the original object.

Making multiple copies in a grid

If you need to clone single or multiple objects, you can use the **Replicate** feature to avoid repetitive copy and paste operations. For example, you can specify three columns and three rows (opposite).

To replicate an object:

1. Select an object. Remember to size the object to be cloned and place it in a convenient starting position—usually the top-left of the page.

2. Choose **Replicate** from the **Tools** menu.

3. In the dialog, set the Grid size by choosing number of columns or rows. Objects are cloned into this grid arrangement (but can be moved subsequently into any position).

4. Set an X and Y spacing (horizontal and vertical gap) between objects if necessary.

5. Click **OK**.

Applying a transform

The Transform feature lets you make multiple copies of one or more selected objects, with a transformation applied to each successive copy in the series.

For example, a butterfly can be made to fly with a transform of 15° rotation, 113% scaling, 4 copies, and an X offset of 1.5cm.

To create a transform:

1. Select an object then choose **Transform** from the **Tools** menu.

2. From the dialog, specify the type of transformation (rotation and/or scaling), the number of copies, and a positional offset between copies.

Copying an object's formatting

Format Painter is used to copy one object's line and fill properties directly to another object, including between line/shape and text objects.

To apply one object's formatting to another:

1. Select the object whose formatting you wish to copy.

2. Click **Format Painter** on the **Standard** toolbar. When you click the button, the selected object's formatting is "picked up".

3. Click another object to apply the first object's formatting to it. The second object becomes selected.

> To cancel Format Painter mode, press **Esc**, click on a blank area, or choose any tool button.

For copy formatting from one text object to another, a number of other text properties (font, font size, and so on) besides line and fill are passed along at the same time.

Moving objects

You can move any selected object anywhere you want and drop it back onto the page or pasteboard by releasing the mouse button.

To move one or more objects:

1. Select the object(s).

2. Click and drag the ⊕ **Move** button. The object moves.

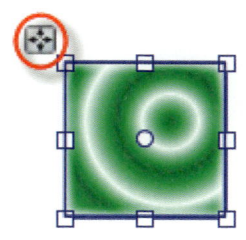

- or -
Click within the selection and drag.

> 💡 Use the keyboard arrows to move in increments.

> 💡 To set exact horizontal and vertical positions, use the Transform tab.

Resizing objects

DrawPlus offers a range of resizing options directly on the object.

Most objects in DrawPlus maintain their aspect ratio when being resized. One exception is when resizing QuickShapes, as their versatility lend themselves to being resized without constraint.

Manipulating Objects

To resize an object to a fixed aspect ratio:

1. Select the object(s) with the **Pointer Tool**.

2. Position the cursor over one of the object's handles—you will notice that the cursor changes to a double-headed Size cursor.

3. Drag from a corner handle (above) to resize in two dimensions (by moving two edges), while maintaining the selection's aspect ratio (proportions).

> To resize to any aspect ratio, with the **Shift** key depressed, drag from an object's corner handle. This resizes in two directions. If you drag an object's side handles, you'll stretch or squash the object in one direction.

To resize QuickShapes:

- As above but the object's aspect ratio is not maintained by default on resize.

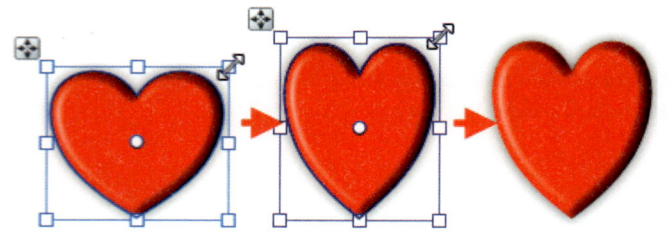

You can use the **Shift** key as you resize to maintain aspect ratio.

Rotating and shearing objects

The **Rotate Tool** lets you both rotate and shear (slant) one or more objects.

To rotate one or more objects around a centre point:

1. Click **Rotate Tool** on the **Drawing** toolbar's Selection flyout.
2. Click to select the object, then hover over a corner handle and, when you see the cursor change, drag in the direction in which you want to rotate the object then release the mouse. (Use **Shift** key for rotating in 15 degree intervals.)

Note that when rotating objects, dimensions will be temporarily displayed during the operation.

To change the centre point of rotation:

1. Move the centre of rotation ○ away from its original position to any position on the page. The marker can also be moved to be outside the object—ideal for rotating grouped objects around a central point.
2. Drag the rotate pointer to a new rotation angle—the object will rotate about the new pivot.

To rotate selected object by set degrees:

- For 90° anti-clockwise: click **Rotate Left 90°** on the **Standard** toolbar.

- For 30°, 45°, 60°, and 90° options left and right, as well as 180°: click the down arrow on the Arrange tab's **Rotate** button and select a value. Once set, clicking the button will rotate the object by the chosen value incrementally.

Besides being able to rotate an object, the Rotate Tool allows you to skew or "shear" it.

To shear or copy shear an object:

1. Select **Rotate Tool** on the **Drawing** toolbar's Selection flyout.

2. Click to select the object(s), hover over any side handle (not a corner handle) until you see the Shear cursor.

3. Hold the mouse down and drag the pointer in the direction in which you want to shear the object, then release.

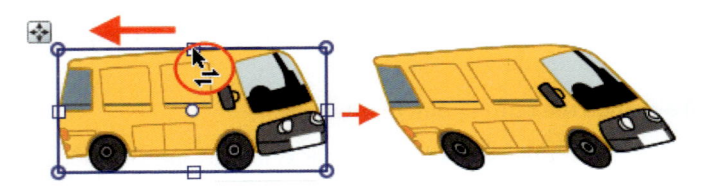

To copy-shear, use the **Ctrl** key while dragging—this preserves the original object, while shearing the new copied object as you drag.

To undo the rotation or shear (restore the original object):

- Double-click the object.

Cutting up objects

It is possible to cut any object (or picture for that matter) by using the **Knife Tool**. You can cut along a freeform or straight line drawn across your object(s), leaving you with separate fragments of the original.

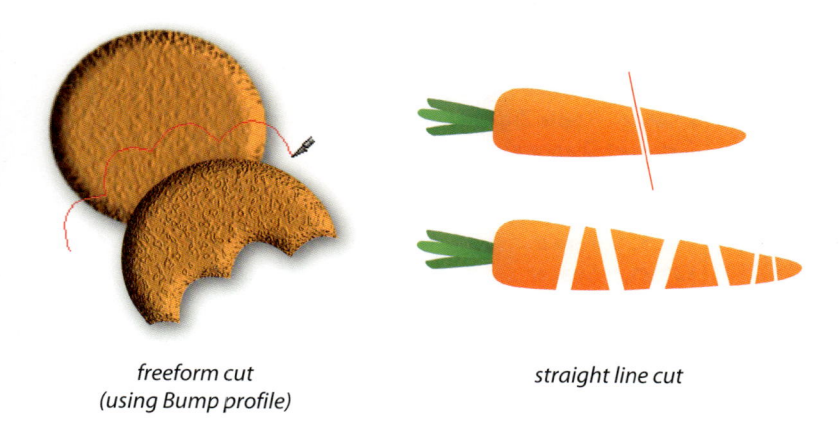

freeform cut (using Bump profile)

straight line cut

To cut selected objects (freeform or straight line):

1. Select the **Knife Tool** on the **Drawing** toolbar's **Vector Edit** flyout.

2. (Optional) Use **Smoothness** on the tool's context toolbar to set how regular the freeform cutting line is—click the right arrow and drag the slider right for increasing smoothness.

3. (Optional) By default, you'll get a straight cutting profile, but for regular-shaped cuts, pick a **Cutting Profile** from the context toolbar.

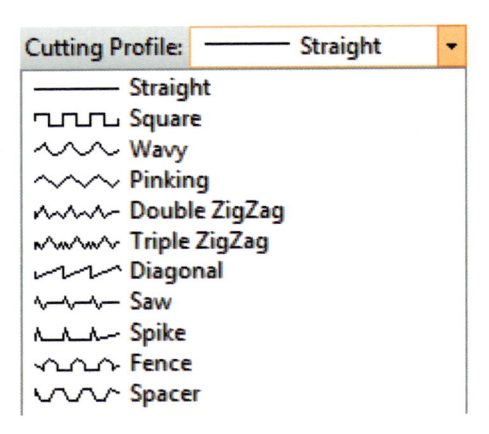

Cutting Profile:	——— Straight ▾
———	Straight
⊓⊔⊓⊔	Square
⌒⌒⌒	Wavy
∧∧∧∧	Pinking
⋀⋀⋀⋀	Double ZigZag
⋀⋀⋀⋀⋀	Triple ZigZag
⌒⌒⌒	Diagonal
⋀⋁⋀⋁	Saw
⋀_⋀_	Spike
⌒⌒⌒	Fence
⌣⌣⌣	Spacer

If required, adjust the **Wavelength** and/or **Amplitude** for your shaped cut.

4. Using the cursor, drag a freeform line across any object(s) you would like to split (unselected objects on which the line traverses will not be split). Instead, press the **Shift** key as you drag for a **straight** line.

5. Hover over, then click to remove the unwanted cut area(s).

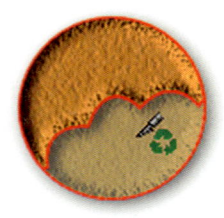

- or -

With the Pointer Tool, drag the newly split fragments apart instead.

Erasing and adding to objects

DrawPlus lets you take a "virtual" eraser to your drawing, letting you **remove** portions of your selected object(s) on an individual layer or across multiple layers. The extent of erasing can be controlled depending on the tool's currently set erasing nib width and pressure setting (if using a graphics tablet).

The flip side of erasing is "**adding to**" (i.e., augmenting), a technique to add or "grow" a vector objects' boundaries—great for reshaping an existing object or to grow a vector shape from scratch. This may be especially useful when creating an unusual filled shape.

To erase portions of a selected object:

1. Select the **Erase Tool** on the **Drawing** toolbar's **Vector Edit** flyout.

2. (Optional) From the context toolbar, choose a **Nib** style (circle, square, or diamond) and/or set a **Width** to define the erase width that will be cut.

3. Position the cursor, and drag over an object boundary (or within an object). You'll see the area to be erased being drawn temporarily (use the **Ctrl** key to redefine the erase area while drawing).

4. Release the mouse button to erase the area drawn.

To add to a selected object:

1. Select the **Freeform Paint Tool** on the **Drawing** toolbar's **Vector Edit** flyout.

2. (Optional) From the context toolbar, set a **Width** to define the nib width which will be drawn.

3. Position the cursor over the object and drag over an object boundary (or within the object). You'll see shading which represents the area to be added. (You can use the **Ctrl** key to redefine the painted area while holding down the mouse button).

4. Release the mouse button to reshape the object to include the newly drawn area.

Joining objects

Objects you create on the page can be just the starting point in your design. For drawn shapes and ready-to-go QuickShapes, it is possible to treat these objects as "building blocks" in the creation of more complex shapes.

The **Shape Builder Tool** can be used to join together any collection of shapes in a fun and intuitive way, without the need for prior selection of shapes.

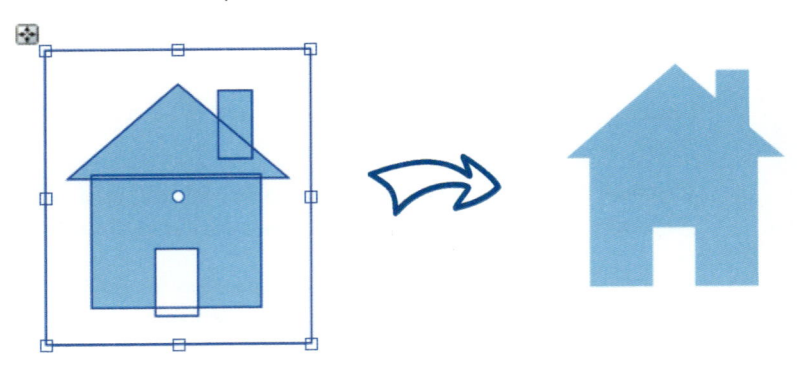

Manipulating Objects **89**

To add shapes together:

1. Select the **Shape Builder Tool** on the **Drawing** toolbar.

2. Hover over a shape that overlaps another shape. You'll see a ⁺ cursor shown on hover over, above a shaded area (to indicate the active region).

3. Drag to the neighbouring shape, using the drawn out dashed line as a guide, then release the mouse button.

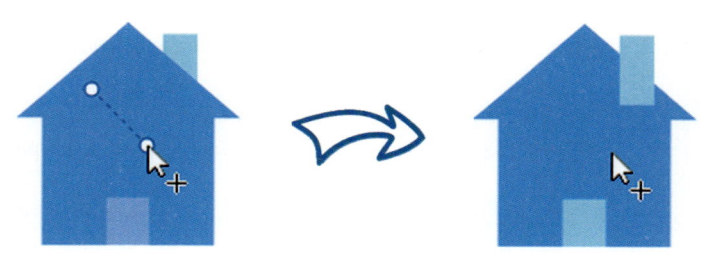

As well as adding objects together, DrawPlus lets you take away (or subtract) intersecting areas of overlapping shapes.

90 *Manipulating Objects*

To subtract intersecting areas:

1. Select the **Shape Builder Tool** on the **Drawing** toolbar.

2. Hover over any intersecting area, then **Alt**-click to remove. You'll see a cursor on hover over.

To create new shapes from overlapped shapes:

1. Select the **Shape Builder Tool** on the **Drawing** toolbar.

2. Click once in the chosen area, then select with the **Pointer Tool** (**Drawing** toolbar). You can then drag the new shape to a new position.

Using the Arrange tab

Instead of using the ShapeBuilder Tool, you have the option of using the selection-based Combine tool or "Join" tools such as Add, Subtract, and Intersect using the Arrange tab. See DrawPlus Help for more information.

8 Arranging Objects

Grouping objects

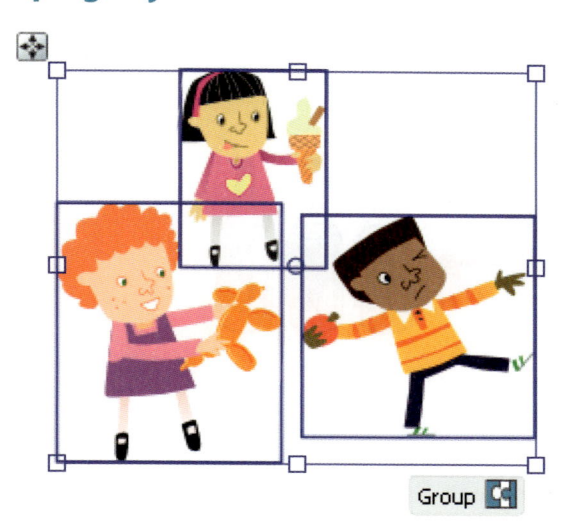

The advantage of converting a set of objects into a group is that it is easier to select and edit the objects all at the same time. The only requirement for grouping is that multiple objects are selected in advance (see p. 27).

To create a group from a multiple selection:

- Click **Group** below the selection.

To ungroup (turn a group back into a multiple selection):

- Click **Ungroup** below the selection.

> Objects within groups can be selected with **Ctrl**-click and edited without having to ungroup your grouped objects.

Aligning and distributing objects

Alignment involves taking a group of selected objects and aligning or distributing them, or both—the operation is applied to all of the objects selected.

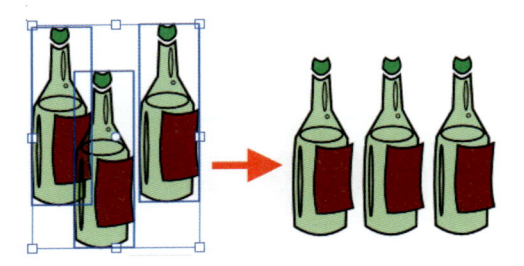

To align two or more objects:

1. Using the **Pointer Tool**, **Shift**-click on all the objects you want to align, or draw a marquee box around them (or use **Edit>Select All**), to create a multiple selection.

2. From the context toolbar, Align tab, or **Arrange>Align Objects**, select an option for vertical alignment or horizontal alignment of an object. Object means the last selected object for **Shift**-click multiple selection or the topmost object in Z-order for marquee multiple selection.

To distribute objects:

1. Using the **Pointer Tool**, **Shift**-click on all the objects you want to distribute, or draw a marquee box around them, to create a multiple selection.

2. Display the Align tab.

3. From the tab, check the **Spaced** option and enter a value in the input box to set distribute objects between a fixed distance.

    - or -

    Check **Include Page** to distribute objects relative to the page edges, instead of between endmost objects.

    - or -

    Check both **Spaced** and **Include Page** to distribute objects between a fixed distance relative to the page edges.

4. Select **Distribute Horizontally** or **Distribute Vertically** to distribute objects vertically or horizontally, respectively.

Ordering objects

Think of the objects on a page as being stacked or piled on top of each other. The front-most object is the one on top of the stack. Each time you create a new object, it goes in front of the objects already there. But you can move any object to any **depth** in the ordering sequence, and obtain sophisticated drawing effects by learning how to manipulate the front/back relationship of objects.

As an example, we've used a camera lens to illustrate ordering.

Notice how the lens possesses a "realistic" look by blending overlapped composite objects.

Gradient and solid fills combine to simulate three-dimensional objects (with reflections, highlights and shading).

To change the selected object's order (dynamically via slider):

- From the Arrange tab, drag the **Depth** slider left to place the object further down the object order (within its layer); drag right to place object further up the order. Ordering occurs as you drag.

To change the selected object's order (via ordering buttons):

- To shift the selected object's position to the front of other objects (on top), choose **Bring to Front** on the **Standard** toolbar (or Arrange tab).

- To shift the selected object's position behind other objects (on the bottom), choose **Send to Back** on the **Standard** toolbar (or Arrange tab).

- ![icon] To shift the object's position one step toward the front, choose **Forward One** on the Arrange tab.

- ![icon] To shift the object's position one step toward the back, choose **Back One** on the Arrange tab.

Working with layers

If you are drawing something simple, you don't really need to make use of layers—you can do all your work on the single layer that every new drawing has. However, if you're creating something a little more tricky then layers can be a vital aid in separating objects into independent sets. You can think of layers as transparent sheets of paper upon which you can draw your objects.

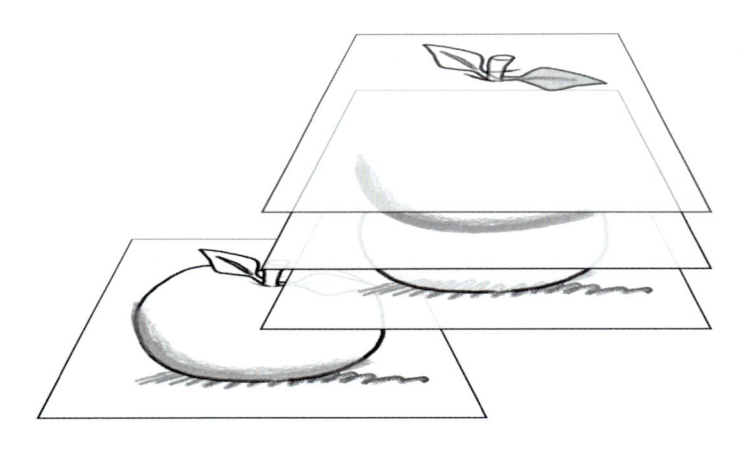

Layers are useful when you're working on a complex design where it makes sense to separate one cluster of objects from another. The whole drawing is produced by piling up the layers and viewing all of the objects on all of the layers; you can choose which layer you are editing and thus make changes without fear of modifying anything on another layer. In essence, by building up your drawing from multiple layers you make it much easier to edit.

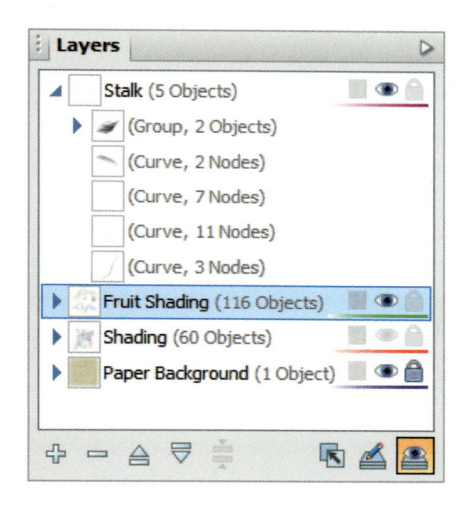

Each layer is situated along with other layers (if present) within a stack on the **Layers tab**—the uppermost layer is applied over any lower layer on the page. You can also expand each layer entry for a tree view of objects associated with that layer (see the Stalk layer opposite). Each object entry can be clicked to select the object in your workspace.

In order to create a new object on a particular layer, you'll first need to "activate" (select) that layer.

To select a particular layer:

- Click a layer name in the Layers tab.

To add a new layer:

- In the Layers tab, click the **Add Layer** button to add a new layer above the currently selected layer.

To rename a layer:

- To rename a layer to something more meaningful, click on the selected layer's name and type to add your new name (you can also make an insertion point to edit the existing text).

To delete a layer:

- In the Layers tab, select the layer's name and click the **Delete Layer** button.

> If you delete a layer, all of the objects on it are lost! So if you want to keep any of them, move them to another layer first.

98 *Arranging Objects*

You can move layers up or down in the stacking order to place their objects in front or behind those on other layers, move objects to specific layers, and even merge layers.

To move a layer in the stacking order:

- Drag the selected layer to a new position in the layer stack.

Remember that objects on layers are drawn in the order in which the layers were initially added to the Layers tab. Put another way: the bottom layer in the Layers tab stack is drawn first then the second bottom, third bottom etc. A background layer should be the bottom layer in the Layers tab stack.

Layer Properties

Layer properties allow you to assign paper textures, make layers invisible/visible, and/or locked/unlocked.

See Studio: Layers tab in DrawPlus Help for more details.

Managing objects on layers

A useful feature of the Layers tab is that you can see objects or even groups of objects, under the layer on which they were created. This gives you the option of selecting an object or group from the tab as opposed to from the page itself. Groups and individual objects can be named, allowing you to more easily locate them in the Layers tab, which in turn locates them in the workspace for you.

To add objects to a particular layer:

- When drawn, objects are added to the selected layer automatically. This is why it is a good idea to check which layer you are currently working on!

Arranging Objects **99**

To select an object on a layer:

1. On the Layers tab, click the ▶ **Expand** icon on the chosen layer entry to reveal all associated objects.

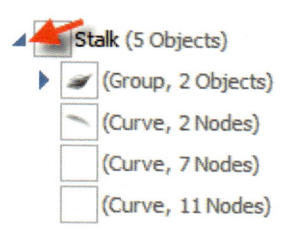

   - Stalk (5 Objects)
     - (Group, 2 Objects)
     - (Curve, 2 Nodes)
     - (Curve, 7 Nodes)
     - (Curve, 11 Nodes)

   This tree view greatly improves the ability to select and manage nested objects in more complex drawings. It's also great for visualizing your object order.

2. Click the object entry in the tab. It will become highlighted and selected on your page.

> Trouble locating your **named** object or group? Search for it by using **Find Object** on the **Edit** menu.

To move an object to another layer:

- Right-click the object in the workspace, and choose **Move Object to Layer**. From the **Move To Layer** dialog, select the specific destination layer, and click **OK**.

To hide/show an object on a layer:

- Right-click the object in the Layers tab (or multiple objects via **Ctrl**-click), and select **Visible**. To show again, click the 👁 icon displayed on the object entry.

9 Fills, Lines, Colours, and Transparency

Setting fill properties

Any closed shape, such as a closed curve or QuickShape, or text has an interior region that can be filled. The fill type can be solid, gradient, bitmap or plasma. Those that use a single colour are solid fills.

Fill types fall into several basic categories, illustrated above:

- **Solid fills**, as their name implies, use a single colour.

- **Gradient fills** provide a gradation or spectrum of colours between two or more "key" colours. Mesh fills work like gradient fills but with a more complex fill path.

- **Bitmap and Plasma fills** apply bitmapped images or patterns to the object, each with unique properties. Think of bitmap fills as named "pictures" that fill shapes. Plasma (or "fractal") fills use randomized patterns, useful for simulating cloud or shadow effects.

Solid colours

Applying a fill is easy, whether you're selecting a colour from the **Colour tab** or the **Swatch tab**.

The **Colour** tab can operate in several modes available from a drop-down list—HSL Colour Wheel (shown), HSL Colour Box, HSL Sliders, RGB Sliders, RGB Sliders (Hex), CMYK Sliders and Tinting.

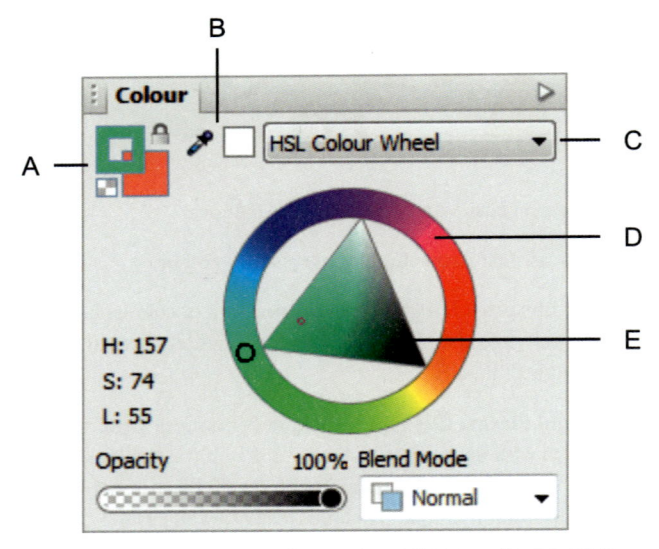

(A) Line/Fill swatches, (B) Colour Picker, (C) Colour Model, (D) Hue wheel, (E) Saturation/Lightness triangle.

On the HSL Colour Wheel, the small circles shown in the wheel and triangle indicate the current setting for hue and saturation/lightness, respectively. Drag either circle around to adjust the values.

The Line/Fill swatches on the tab govern whether the selected colour is applied as a line colour, solid fill, or both simultaneously.

By comparison, the **Swatch** tab hosts a vast array of preset colour swatches for solid, gradient, plasma, and bitmap fills. Swatches are stored in palettes which can be managed from within the tab. You can even create your own palettes and palette categories.

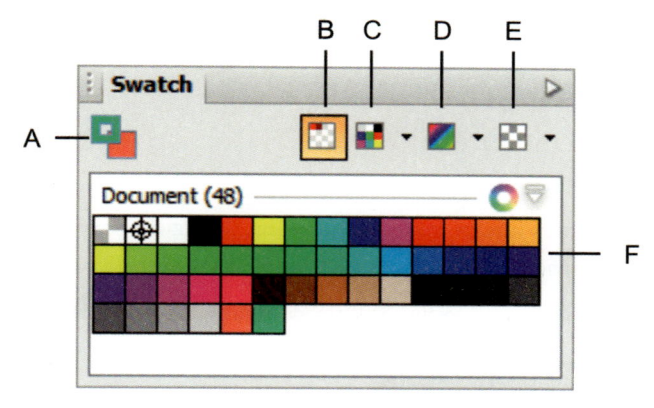

*(**A**) Line/Fill swatches, (**B**) Document Palette, (**C**) Standard and themed palettes, (**D**) Gradient palettes, (**E**) Bitmap palettes, (**F**) Current palette.*

CMYK operation

If you intend to create professional CMYK output to PDF or image, you can optionally create a CMYK drawing from scratch (see p. 14). Your drawing, in a CMYK colour space, can be designed using CMYK colours (instead of RGB colours) either using:

- **CMYK Sliders**. (Click the colour model drop-down list on the Colour tab.)

    - or -

- **Standard CMYK Palette**. (Click the **Palettes** button on the Swatch tab.)

Applying colour

To apply a solid fill colour via the Colour tab:

1. Select the object(s) and display the Studio's **Colour tab**.

2. Click the Line/Fill Swatch at the top-left of the tab so the Fill Swatch appears in front of the Line swatch.

    This defines where the colour will be applied. Alternatively, apply colour to both line and fill simultaneously by clicking **Link** on the swatch.

3. (Optional) Choose a colour display mode from the drop-down list.

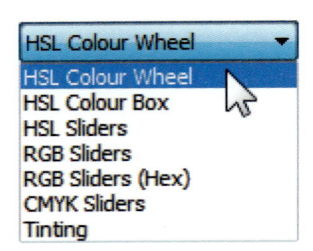

4. Select a colour from the display.

To apply a solid fill colour via the Swatch tab:

1. Select the object(s) and display the Studio's **Swatch tab**.

2. Set the Line/Fill Swatch at the top-left of the tab so the Fill Swatch appears in front of the Line Swatch.

3. Pick a thumbnail from either the **Document Palette** or from another palette shown in the **Palettes** drop-down list (drag from the thumbnail onto the object as an alternative).

A **Tinting** option in the Colour tab's drop-down list allows a percentage of shade/tint to be applied to your colour.

To change a fill's shade/tint (lightness):

1. Select the object and set the Line/Fill Swatch as described for the Colour tab above.

2. From the tab's colour mode drop-down list, select **Tinting**.

3. Drag the slider to the left or right to darken or lighten your starting colour, respectively (the original colour is set at 0%).

You can also enter a percentage value in the box (entering 0 or dragging the pointer back to its original position reverts to the original colour).

To apply a gradient, bitmap, or plasma fill to one or more objects:

As for applying a solid colour fill with the **Swatch** tab but:

- Instead of using a solid colour palette, pick a relevant category from the **Gradient** or **Bitmap** galleries, and pick your required thumbnail from the displayed presets (drag from the thumbnail onto the deselected object as an alternative).

For solid, gradient or plasma fills, you can then edit **colour(s) and shade/tint** (lightness). For gradient and plasma fills, the fill **path** (coverage) can also be edited (see Working with gradient fills on p. 116).

To edit an object's fill colour(s) and tint:

1. Right-click the object and choose **Format>Fill**.

2. (Optional) From the dialog's **Model** drop-down list, choose a different colour model (e.g., RGB sliders).

3. Depending on the selected colour mode, use the Colour Wheel, Colour Picker, or combination of slider and colour spectrum (or use the input boxes) to set your colour value. When using the colour spectrum, click anywhere in the window then drag the marker around to fine-tune your colour selection.

4. Click **OK**.

> An **Opacity** level can be applied to your fill at the same time that a colour is applied; this leads to powerful colour/opacity combinations on solid fills, or on gradient and plasma fill paths. (See Setting opacity on p. 124.)
>
> For gradient or bitmap transparency effects (see p. 128), use the Transparency Tool or Transparency tab.

To apply no fill:

Set an empty interior for objects by using the:

- **Colour tab**: Click **None** in the bottom-left corner of the Line/Fill Swatch, which represents either None (an empty interior for objects with line/fill properties) or Original (for pictures only, to reset the object to its original colours).

  - or -

- **Swatch tab**: Choose the first swatch, **None**, from any gallery.

Blend modes

The **Colour** tab hosts a **Blend Mode** drop-down list for blending overlapping object colours together in various ways. You'll find blend modes described in Understanding blend modes on p. 123.

Setting line properties

All lines, including those that enclose shapes, have numerous properties, including colour, style, line ends, width, join (corner), and cap (end).

Using the Studio's Line tab, you can adjust **plain line** properties for any freeform, straight, or curved line, as well as for the edge of a shape, image or artistic text.

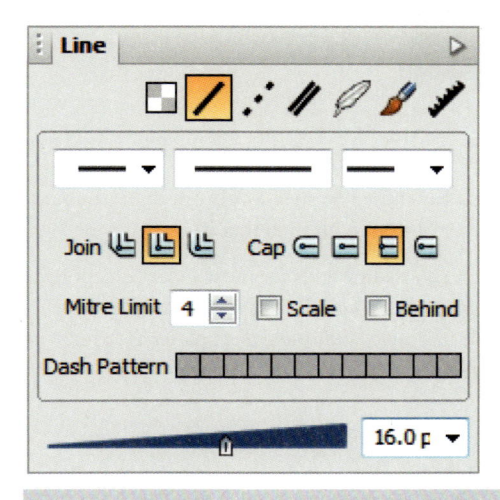

> To change line colour, see Setting fill properties on p. 103.

Changing line style

A series of buttons arranged along the top of the Line tab set the line style.

No line, **Solid**, **Dash**, **Double**, and **Calligraphic** styles can be applied to freeform lines, and outlines of shapes, images and artistic text alike.

The additional two line effects, **Brush Stroke** and **Edge Effect,** let you apply a brush (stroke, spray or edge) effect to the outlines of artistic text, images or objects. You can see your current brush in the Line tab and select a new brush from the Brushes tab. **Brush Stroke** styles can also be added to freeform lines.

To change line style:

- Simply click a button to set the line style—only one style can be set any one time. Pick another button to jump to that style.

Once a style is selected you can choose line ends for most styles (except Brush Stroke and Edge Effect). For some styles, variations are also available. For example, for a Dash or Double line style, additional dash patterns (below) and double line options can be selected.

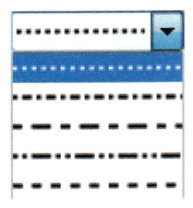

To select a line end:

- From the [────▼] drop-down lists, pick a line start and end.

Other styles such as Dash and Calligraphic offer further customization of the chosen style.

Changing line caps and joins

The Line tab also lets you vary a line's **Cap** (end) and **Join** (corner) where two lines intersect. Both properties tend to be more conspicuous on thicker lines; joins are more apparent with more acute angles.

Changing line width

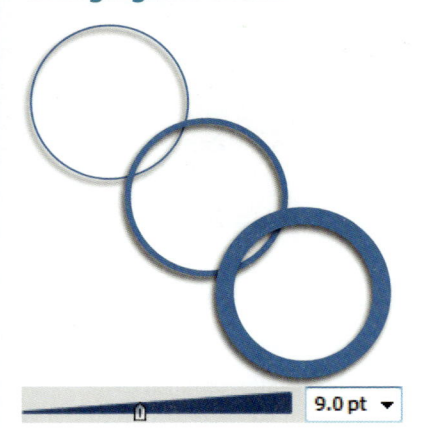

On a selected line, curve, or shape (opposite), drag the **Width** slider in the Line tab. To turn off the line, set the box to 0pt.

Sampling colours

Use the **Colour Picker Tool** to sample (and then reuse) a colour from anywhere on your page. The picked colour can then be made the current line or fill colour in DrawPlus.

Various sampling methods can be used depending on the type of object fill or screen area to be sampled.

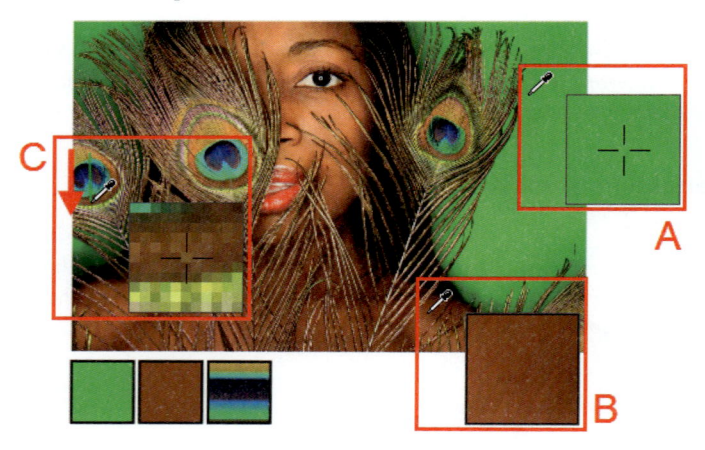

- **Point sampler (A)**
  Use for picking up an individual pixel colour directly under the cursor.

- **Square/circle sampler (B)**
  Use for sampling halftone images, dithered GIFs, or images with varying colour artefacts. The colours within the shaped outlined region in the magnification area are **averaged**, rather than using a specific pixel colour.

  Use a square or circle shape depending on the shape of the region to be sampled.

- **Gradient sampler (C)**
  Use for picking up colour gradients present in images.

Fills, Lines, Colours, and Transparency **113**

To sample colours:

1. On the Drawing toolbar, click **Colour Picker**.

2. From the context toolbar, choose a **Colour Picker Type** (e.g., Point Sampler).

   Point Sampler Square Sampler Circle Sampler Gradient Sampler

3. (Optional) If you use the Square or Circle Sampler, set a **Colour Picker Size** appropriate to the area you want to sample.

   Gradient Sampler offers a **Gradient Picker Sensitivity** option, for controlling the level or detail to which the gradient is sampled.

4. Hold the mouse button down, and drag to the target area then release. For gradient sampling, rather than clicking, you sample by dragging a line across your chosen colour gradient.

   The sampled colour(s) is picked up in the Colour tab's **Picked Colour** swatch.

5. Click the Colour tab's **Line** or **Fill** swatch, then the Picked Colour swatch to transfer the colour to the chosen swatch. You can then apply the colour to any object (this will then be stored automatically in the Swatch tab's Document Palette for further use).

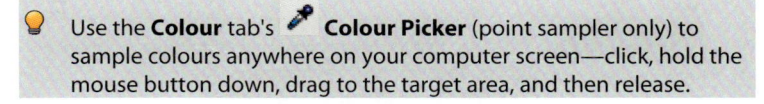

> Use the **Colour** tab's **Colour Picker** (point sampler only) to sample colours anywhere on your computer screen—click, hold the mouse button down, drag to the target area, and then release.

114 *Fills, Lines, Colours, and Transparency*

Defining line and fill colours

When you're applying a **fill** or **line colour** using the Studio's Swatch tab, you choose a colour from one of several colour **palettes**, arranged as a gallery of colour swatch thumbnails. Different palettes can be loaded but only one palette is displayed at any one time.

Several of the colour palettes are based on "themed" colours while the remaining palettes are based on industry-standard colour models, i.e.

- **Standard RGB**: Red, Green and Blue (default).
- **Standard CMYK**: Cyan, Magenta, Yellow and Black. (For professional PDF or image printing, optionally from a CMYK drawing.)

Applying a colour from any of the above palettes to an object will add that to DrawPlus's **Document Palette**, a set of colours currently in use (or previously used) in your document (plus standard colours). The Document Palette is primarily used to reuse colours already in your drawing—great for working to a specific "tailored" set of colours.

To complement the default standard colours (**A**) in the Swatch tab's Document Palette, you can also store (**B**) other palette colours, (**C**) bitmap fills, (**D**) gradient/plasma/mesh fills, (**E**) colour spreads, and (**F**) colours generated from pictures.

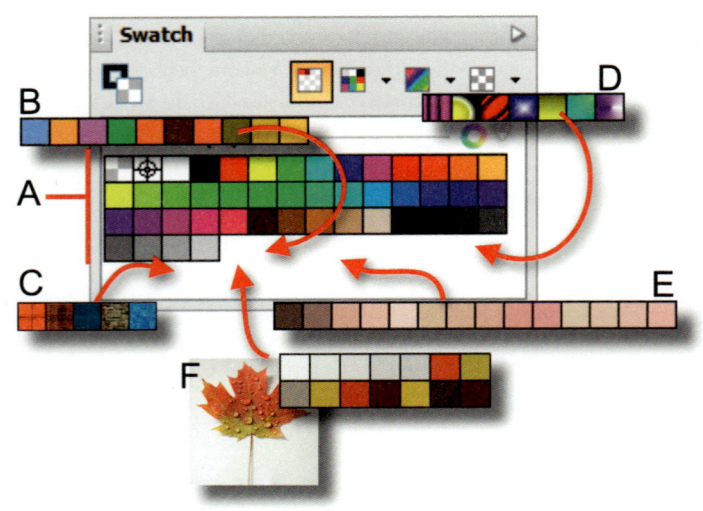

Adding colours to the Document Palette

Colours are added manually or automatically from the Colour tab or taken directly from an object's line/fill into the user's **Document Palette**.

The palette also stores commonly used colours (e.g., Red, Green, Blue, etc.).

Colours can be added, edited, deleted, or renamed within the Document Palette as in any of the other Swatch tab's palettes.

Colours in the Document Palette are just saved locally, along with the drawing's current defaults. That is, the colours don't automatically carry over to new drawings. However, changes to the other palettes are saved globally, making them available to all drawings.

To add a colour to the Document Palette (from Colour tab):

- Select a colour mixed from the Colour tab.

If the colour doesn't already exist in the Swatch tab's Document Palette, a new thumbnail appears for it.

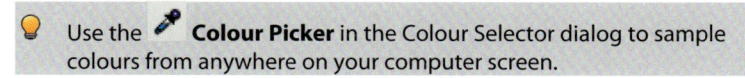

> Use the **Colour Picker** in the Colour Selector dialog to sample colours from anywhere on your computer screen.

To add a colour to the Document Palette manually:

1. Select a different palette (themed, gradient, or bitmap palette).
2. Right-click a palette swatch and select **Add to Document's Palette**.

To add colour spreads (using Colour Palette Designer):

1. Click **Colour Palette Designer** on the Document Palette's title bar.
2. Choose a **Base Colour**, a **Spread** (from the drop-down list), and click either the **Add Range** or **Add All** button.
3. Click **OK**.

For more details, see Creating colour palettes from spreads in DrawPlus Help.

To add colours from a selected picture:

1. On the Picture context toolbar, click **Generate Palette**.
2. From the Palette Creator, select a **Profile** for a small to larger set of generated colours.
3. Click **Create**, then **OK**.

For more details, see Creating colour palettes from pictures in DrawPlus Help.

Adding fills to the Document Palette

To add a solid colour, gradient, mesh, or plasma fill (from a selected object):

1. Click **Palette Menu** and select **Add Fill from Selection**.
2. In the dialog, choose a name and click **OK**.

To add a bitmap fill (from an imported picture):

1. Click **Palette Menu** and select **Add Bitmap Fill**.
2. In the dialog, navigate to the bitmap, select the file name, and click **Open**.

Working with gradient fills

Gradient fills are those that use small "spectrums" with colours spreading between at least two defined **key** values. Specifically, gradient fills can be **linear**, **radial**, **elliptical**, **conical**, **square**, **three colour**, and **four colour** types.

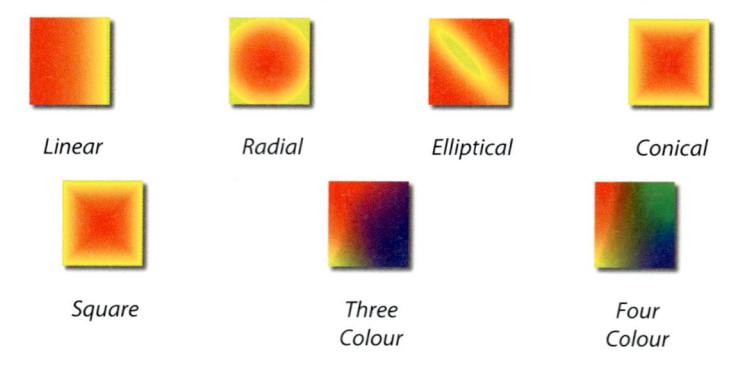

Linear   *Radial*   *Elliptical*   *Conical*

Square   *Three Colour*   *Four Colour*

Applying a gradient fill

There are several ways to apply a gradient fill as a line colour or object fill: using the Fill Tool or via the Swatch tab. Using the Fill Tool, you can vary the fill's path on an object for different effects.

To apply a gradient fill (Fill Tool):

1. Select an object.

2. Click the **Fill Tool** on the **Drawing** toolbar.

3. Click and drag on the object to define the fill path (a solid line). The object takes a simple linear fill, grading from the current colour of the object, ending in white (objects filled with white will grade from white to black, to show contrast).

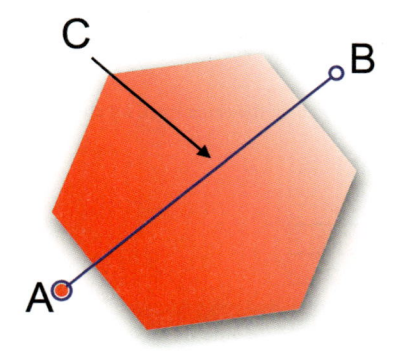

*(**A**) Start Handle colour, (**B**) End Handle colour, and (**C**) Fill Path*

4. To alter the gradient fill colours, change the **Start Colour** and/or **End Colour** on the Fill context toolbar.

From the Swatch tab, automatic fills let you apply a gradient fill (Linear, Radial, Elliptical, or Conical) which dynamically change depending on the colour of a selected object's solid fill or Start/End handles.

To apply a gradient fill (Swatch tab):

1. Select an object.

2. Click the Swatch tab and choose a line or fill colour. Ensure the **Line** or **Fill** swatch is set accordingly.

3. From the Swatch tab, click the **Gradient** button. The Automatic palette appears.

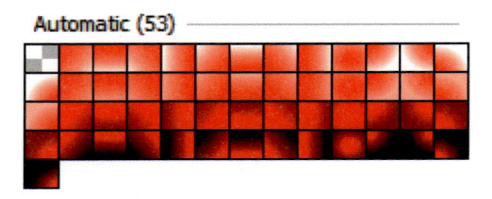

4. From the Automatic category, click the thumbnail for the fill you want to apply.

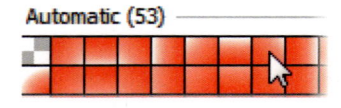

> Other gradient fills are available by clicking the drop-down arrow on the **Gradient** button.

Editing the fill path

You can use the **Fill Tool** to edit the object's **fill path**, defining the placement of the spectrum across the object.

If an object using a gradient fill is selected, you'll see the **fill path** displayed as one or more lines, with circular handles marking where the spectrum between each key colour begins and ends. Adjusting the handle positions determines the actual spread of colours between handles. You can also edit the fill by adding, deleting, or changing key colours.

To adjust the gradient fill path on a selected object:

1. Select an object with a gradient fill.

2. Click **Fill Tool** on the **Drawing** toolbar. The object's fill path appears.

3. Use the Fill Tool to drag the start and end circular path handles, or drag on (or outside) the object for a new start handle, creating a new fill path as you drag. The gradient starts where you place the start handle, and ends where you place the end handle.

    - or -

    Use the Fill context toolbar to **Rotate Left** or **Rotate Right** your fill (in 90 degree increments).

4. From the Fill context toolbar, change the **Start Colour** and/or **End Colour**.

For details of how to edit and manage gradient fills, see DrawPlus Help.

Editing the fill spectrum

Whether you're editing a fill that's already been applied to an object, or redefining one of the gallery fills, the basic concepts are the same. Whereas solid fills use a single colour, all gradient fills utilize at least two "key" colours, with a spread of hues in between each key colour, creating a "spectrum" effect.

You can either edit the fill spectrum directly using the **Fill Tool** or use **Format>Fill** (to access the Fill Editor dialog). With the Fill Tool selected, colours can be selected from the Studio's Colour or Swatch tab to replace a selected handle's colour, or dragged from the Swatch tab to create new handles on the fill path). Both methods let you define key colours. The Fill Tool method is more convenient for this, but with the dialog you can also fine-tune the actual spread of colour between pairs of key colours.

The editing of gradient fills is a complex operation and is covered in greater detail in the DrawPlus Help.

Working with bitmap and plasma fills

A **bitmap fill** uses a named bitmap—often a material, pattern, or background image. DrawPlus supplies an impressive selection of preset bitmap fills on the Swatch tab, and you can import your own.

A **plasma fill**, sometimes called a fractal fill, is a bitmapped pattern with dark and light regions, useful for simulating cloud or shadow effects. Again, the Swatch tab hosts a selection of these fills.

Once you've applied either type of fill to an object using the Swatch tab (see Setting fill properties on p. 103), you can adjust the fill's tint with the Shade/Tint slider in the Colour tab (use Colour mode drop-down list), and use the Fill Tool to edit the object's **fill path**, defining the placement of the fill across the object.

For details of how to edit and manage bitmap and plasma fills, see DrawPlus Help.

Fills, Lines, Colours, and Transparency **121**

Working with mesh fills

A **mesh fill** works using a grid or "mesh" of many nodes representing separate key colours. The overall effect, especially useful for multifaceted highlighting, arises from the colour gradients that spread between each of these nodes.

As an example, the **Mesh Fill Tool** can be used to dramatic effect on a sports car's bodywork.

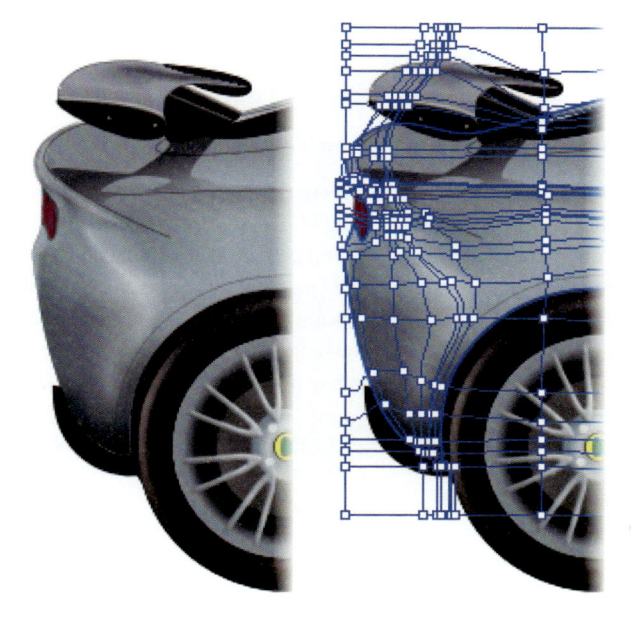

To enable the Mesh Fill Tool:

- Select **Mesh Fill Tool** on the **Drawing** toolbar's Fill flyout. With the tool enabled, a mesh of editable patches and nodes are revealed (above).

122 Fills, Lines, Colours, and Transparency

A mesh fill is applied to an object via the Swatch tab's Gradient gallery (see Setting fill properties on p. 103) . You can edit the mesh itself with the Mesh Fill Tool and the accompanying context toolbar to achieve unique results.

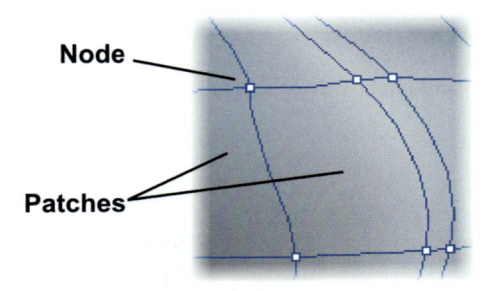

(A) Node and (B) Patches in a mesh fill

The path lines that connect nodes in a mesh fill are actually curves, so editing the mesh is similar to the method for Editing lines and shapes (see p. 43). Simple warping effects, colour spread changes and path line curvature can all be affected. The tool lets you reshape curved path lines by adjusting one or more nodes and their control handles. In addition, the areas between four nodes called "mesh patches" can be recoloured or moved individually or in multiples. As for curved lines you can add, delete, and move one or more nodes at any time.

> Deleting a node also deletes segments and nodes connected to it. If you delete a corner or edge node, the overall mesh area will decrease.

Understanding blend modes

You can think of **blend modes** as different rules for combining pixels to create a resulting colour. Note that blend modes work in relation to the colours of the objects themselves (shapes, lines, brush strokes, and so on).

They are used for **creative effects** on overlapping objects, where colours blend on top of one another. Blend modes can be applied to both a top object's line and fill colour. You can adjust the blend mode of an existing object (brush stroke, etc.) on your page, or you can set the blend mode before creating a brush stroke, line, shape, etc.

For professional design, you can also make use of **composite blend modes**, or **isolated blending** within a group to prevent underlying objects from being affected by the blending operation.

To apply a blend mode to an existing object:

1. Select an existing object on your page.
2. On the Colour tab, choose a blend mode from the **Blend Mode** drop-down list.

To apply a blend mode to a new brush stroke, line, or shape:

1. Select the brush, line, or shape tool you want to use, and set its appropriate settings—width, colour, etc.
2. On the Colour tab, choose a blend mode from the **Blend Mode** drop-down list.
3. Create your stroke, line, or shape on your page.

For a complete list of blend modes, with supporting examples, please see the topic "Understanding blend modes" in DrawPlus help.

Setting opacity

> 💡 **Key point!** In DrawPlus, **opacity** is a property of colour, and can be set directly from the Colour tab. **Transparency** refers to object-based gradient or bitmap transparency effects, set via the Transparency tab or Transparency Tool.

Opacity is great for highlights, shading and shadows, and simulating "rendered" realism. It can make the difference between flat, ordinary visuals and sparkling realism!

Opacity is the inverse of transparency—fully opaque (100%) is no transparency (0%), and vice versa. It works rather like fills that use "disappearing ink" instead of colour. The less opacity in a particular spot, the more "disappearing" takes place there, and the more the object(s) underneath show through.

Butterflies showing 100% opacity, 50% opacity, and 25% opacity (from left to right).

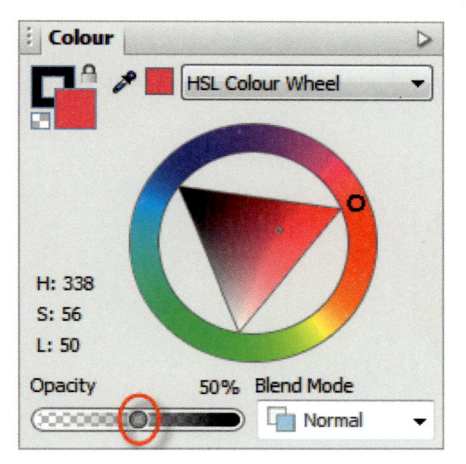

The **Opacity** slider (Colour tab) can be used to alter the opacity of a specific colour, whether that colour is a solid fill (in an object or on a line), or a handle's colour on a gradient fill path. Opacity can be applied locally to each object; the default is 100% opacity, i.e. the object is fully opaque.

For solid fills, the opacity change will be made uniformly across the object's interior (as above). However, for gradient fill paths, different opacity levels can be assigned with colour to handles along the fill path. The combination of different colours and semi-transparency allow interesting colour blends to be made.

> Gradient fill paths are explained in detail in Working with gradient fills on p. 116.

To apply solid opacity:

1. Select the object.
2. From the Studio's **Colour tab**, drag the slider to the left for a reduced **Opacity** setting (e.g., 20%); drag right to increase opacity. This makes objects appear semi-transparent, or if set to 0%, fully transparent.

126 Fills, Lines, Colours, and Transparency

To apply solid opacity (to a fill path):

1. Select the object with a gradient fill and display the Studio's **Colour tab**.

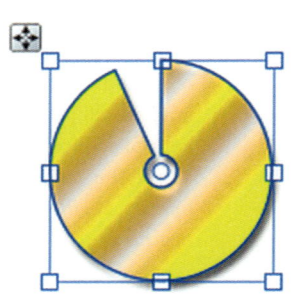

2. Click the **Fill Tool** on the **Drawing** toolbar's Fill flyout. The fill path is displayed.

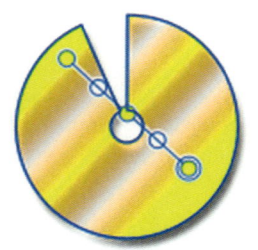

   Click on any displayed handle along the fill path (the handle with a double outline is selected. Use **Shift**-select for selecting multiple handles.

3. From the Colour tab, drag the slider to the left for a reduced opacity setting. You'll notice the new opacity setting influencing the fill's appearance.

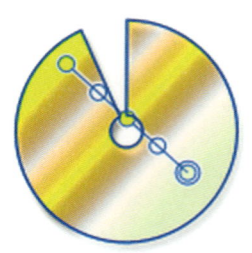

Composite opacity

An individual object can take a specific opacity setting. However, when multiple objects are grouped, the group can be given a **composite opacity**, affecting all group objects to the same extent.

Using transparency effects

While uniform opacity can be applied along with colour via the Colour tab (see Setting opacity on p. 124), it's possible to apply gradient transparency via the Transparency tab or Transparency Tool independent of colour. Bitmap transparency can also be applied exclusively via the Transparency tab.

Just as a gradient fill can vary from light to dark, a gradient transparency varies from more to less transparent, i.e. from clear to opaque. Picking a linear transparency preset from the Transparency tab, and applying it to a shape, shows the transparency effect.

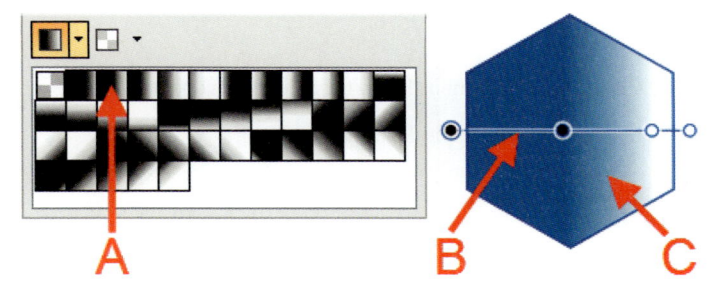

*(**A**) Linear Transparency, (**B**) Transparency path, (**C**) Effect on graphic*

Transparency can also be applied along a custom drawn transparency path using the Transparency Tool, in the same way as the equivalent fill path (see DrawPlus Help). Transparency paths are easily editable.

> Transparency effects are applied locally to each object. Applying different transparency effects won't alter the object's fill settings as such, but may significantly alter a fill's actual appearance.

Let's check out the Transparency tab. As with the Swatch tab, there are galleries for both gradient and bitmap transparencies.

To apply gradient or bitmap transparency effects:

1. With your object selected, go to the Transparency tab.

2. For gradient or bitmap transparency, click the drop down arrow on the **Gradient** or **Bitmap** button, respectively. Select a category from the flyout, then click a thumbnail in that category.

   - or -

   Drag the desired thumbnail from the gallery to an object.

3. The transparency is applied to the object(s).

> Sometimes objects of a lighter colour will not display their transparency clearly—ensure the transparency is applied correctly by temporarily placing the object over a strong solid colour.

Fills, Lines, Colours, and Transparency **129**

To apply gradient transparency with Transparency Tool:

1. Select an object.

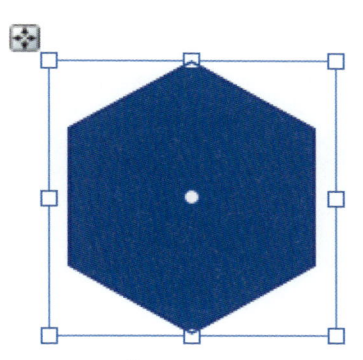

2. Click the **Transparency Tool** on the **Drawing** toolbar.

3. Click and drag on the object to define the transparency path. The object takes a simple linear transparency, grading from 0% transparency (100% opaque) to 100% transparency (0% opaque) in the direction you drag.

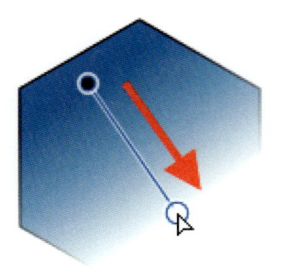

You've freeform control over where the path starts and ends, and the direction in which the path will be drawn. You can even click again to redraw the path.

Editing gradient transparency

Once you've applied a transparency, you can adjust its **path** on the object, and the **level** of transparency along the path. You can even create more complex transparency effects by adding extra handles to the path and assigning different levels to each handle. For details of how to edit and manage gradient transparency, see DrawPlus Help.

> 💡 You cannot alter the values in a bitmap transparency.

10 Pictures

Importing pictures

Targa Bitmap (*.TGA)
Windows Bitmap (*.bmp,*.rle)
Raw files (*.raw,...)
AutoCAD Drawing (*.dwg)
AutoCAD DXF (*.dxf)
Windows Enhanced Metafile (*.emf)
Encapsulated Postscript (*.eps,*.ps)
Graphic Interchange Format (*.gif)
JPEG 2000 (*.j2k,*.jp2)
JPEG File (*.jpg,*.jpe,*.jpeg,*.jfif)
PC PaintBrush (*.pcx)
Portable Network Graphics (*.png)
Adobe Photoshop Image (*.psd)
Paint Shop Pro files (*.psp,*.tub,*.rfr,*
Sun Raster (*.ras,*.sun)
Serif Metafile Format (*.smf)
Serif PhotoPlus Picture (*.spp)
Scalable Vector Graphics (*.svg)
Compressed SVG (*.svgz)
Tagged Image File Format (*.tif,*.tiff)
HD Photo (*.wdp,*.hdp)
Windows Metafile (*.wmf)

A wide range of picture formats can be imported directly into DrawPlus, including vector graphics and metafiles.

Any imported picture ends up as an object you can select, move, scale, shear, rotate—and even cut or crop using the **Knife** or **Crop Tool** on the **Drawing** toolbar. The Image Cutout Studio lets you cut the subject of your picture out from its background (and vice versa).

To import a picture from a file:

1. Click **Insert Picture** on the **Drawing** toolbar.

2. From the **Open** dialog, locate and select the file to import, then click **Open**.

   The dialog disappears and the mouse pointer changes to the Picture Size cursor. What you do next determines the initial size, placement, and aspect ratio (proportions) of the picture.

3. Insert the picture at a default size by simply clicking the mouse.
   - or -
   Set the size of the inserted picture by dragging out a region and releasing the mouse button. By default, the picture's aspect ratio is preserved. To allow free dragging to any aspect ratio, hold down the

If you want to import multiple pictures simultaneously, you can select a range of pictures from within the **Open** dialog. Each image can then be added to the page selectively from a **Picture List** flyout.

Using Cutout Studio

Cutout Studio offers a powerful integrated solution for cutting objects out from their backgrounds. Depending on the make up of your images you can separate subject of interests from their backgrounds, either by retaining the subject of interest (usually people, objects, etc.) or removing a simple uniform background (e.g., sky, studio backdrop). In both instances, the resulting "cutout" image creates an eye-catching look for your design.

An initial image on a coloured background.

Cutout Studio "paints" transparency on the background. The tint indicates areas to be discarded.

Once cut out, a different image can be used as a more attractive background.

To launch Cutout Studio:

1. Select an image to be cut out.

2. Select **Cutout Studio** from the context toolbar. Cutout Studio is launched.

Choose an output

You can choose an output type prior to selecting areas for keeping/discarding, either an alpha-edged or vector-cropped bitmap from the **Output Type** drop-down list. Choose the latter for more well-defined edges.

Selecting areas to keep or discard

A pair of brushes for keeping and discarding is used to enable parts of the image to be selected. The tools are called **Keep Brush** and **Discard Brush**, and are either used independently or, more typically, in combination with each other.

To select image areas for keeping/discarding:

1. In Cutout Studio, click either **Keep brush** or **Discard brush** from the left of the Studio workspace.

2. (Optional) Pick a **Brush size** suitable for the area to be worked on.

3. (Optional) Set a **Grow Tolerance** value to automatically expand the selected area under the cursor (by detecting colours similar to those within the current selection). The greater the value the more the selected area will grow.

4. Using the circular cursor, click and drag across the area to be retained. It's OK to repeatedly click and drag until your selection area is made—you can't lose your selection unless you click the **Reset** button. The **Undo** button reverts to the last made selection.

5. If you're outputting an alpha-edged bitmap, you can refine the area to be kept/discarded within Cutout Studio (only after previewing) with Erase and Restore touch-up tools. Vector-cropped images can be cropped using standard DrawPlus crop tools outside of the Studio.

6. Click **OK** to create your cutout, or **Cancel** to abort the operation.

You'll see your image on the page in its original location, but with the selected areas cut away (made transparent).

Autotracing

Instead of manually tracing a design, it's possible to automatically convert bitmaps into vector objects by using **autotracing**. Its main function is for speedily reworking bitmapped **logos** (for further design modification), but its use is not confined to this. In fact, both greyscale and colour **photos** can equally be autotraced for eye-catching artistic effects.

For each of these uses, DrawPlus offers a studio environment and a specific preset profile which will produce optimum results while autotracing artwork of your chosen type.

- **B/W Image Trace**. For black and white tracings of photos, scanned images, and line drawings.

- **Logo Image Trace**. For tracing pictures such as logos, signatures, or other designs with antialiasing.

- **Photo Image Trace**. For colour tracing of photos.

To autotrace a selected image:

1. Click the drop-down arrow on the **AutoTrace** button (on context toolbar) and select a profile from the menu.
   - or -

   Click **AutoTrace** and choose a profile from the profile selection screen.

2. The AutoTrace studio appears with the original artwork displayed, along with adjustable sliders, a colour palette (logo profile only), or a collapsible preview window (photo profiles only) showing how your output will look once traced.

3. (Optional) Adjust the sliders at the right of the workspace (each unique to the profile used); your profile settings will be modified.

4. Click **Trace** to trace your logo, photo, or other bitmapped artwork. It's best to keep clicking this button to update your main window after any adjustment. If you want to abort the autotracing process, you can click the **Cancel** button on the progress bar.

5. (Optional) For fine-tuning your traced output, several options are possible:

    - Click **Adjust** to access **Merge**, **Fill**, and **Node tools** for fine-tuning your vector output.

    - For removing colours in traced logo output, right-click on the palette colour you want to remove.

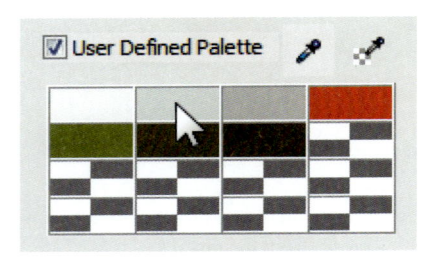

    You can **add** a new colour or **replace** an existing colour by left-clicking on an empty or occupied colour swatch and dragging the **Colour Selector** to any colour on your computer screen. Remember to click **Trace** to refresh the view.

6. When you're happy with your traced output, click **Accept**.

> All slider settings are described in full in the Help pane which accompanies the AutoTrace studio. Also covered are procedures for tracing greyscale and colour photos.

The autotracing procedure above differs slightly when applied to greyscale or colour photos, i.e. instead of comprehensive palette control you have a photo preview.

Applying PhotoLab filters

PhotoLab is a dedicated studio environment that lets you apply adjustment and effect filters to photos, individually or in combination.

Photos present in your drawing display in the **Images** tab, which is hidden by default. To display this tab, as illustrated below, simply click the ▬▬▲▬▬ button at the bottom of the dialog.

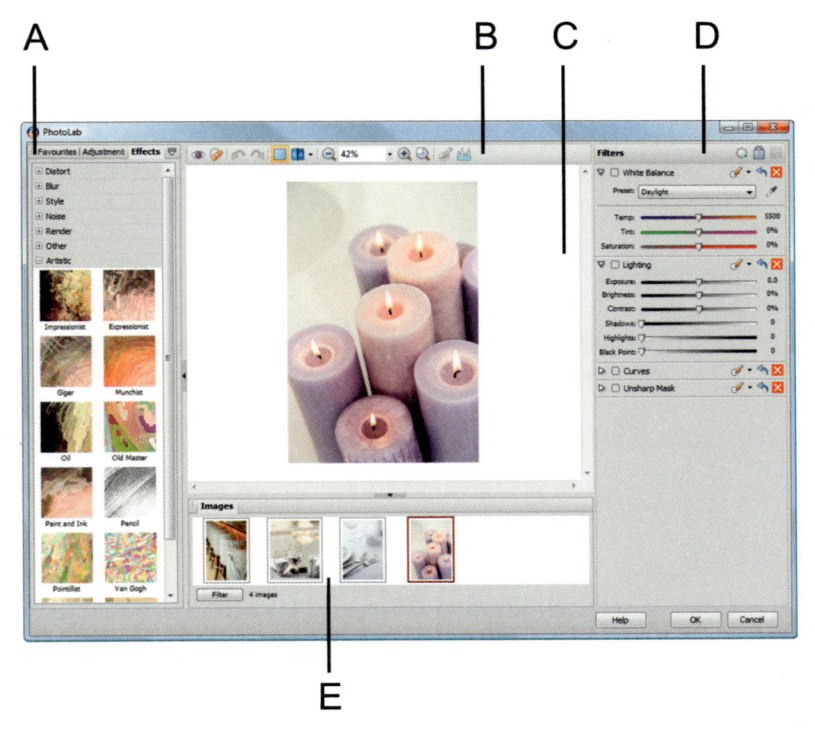

(A) filter tabs, (B) Main toolbar, (C) Main workspace, (D) filter stack, (E) Images tab

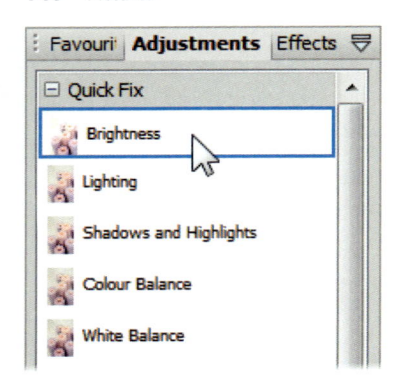

Filters are stored in the **Favourites**, **Adjustments**, and **Effects** filter tabs, and are grouped into categories.

For example, the **Adjustments** tab provides the **Quick Fix** and **Pro Edit** categories, while the **Effects** tab offers a wide range of creative effect categories.

> You can add your own custom filters to the Favourites tab. (See DrawPlus Help.)

Applying filters

1. Select the photo you want to work on. (If the photo is framed, select it and click **Select Cropped Object**.)

2. Click **PhotoLab** on the context toolbar.

3. For ease of use, when you open PhotoLab, the **Filters** stack on the right contains some commonly-used filters (such as **White Balance** and **Lighting**). These filters are disabled by default.

   To apply one of the default filters, click its **Enable/Disable** control to enable it, and then adjust the filter settings by dragging the sliders.

   To disable, reset, and delete a filter, see DrawPlus Help.

To add a new filter:

1. Browse the filter thumbnails displayed on the **Favourites**, **Adjustments**, and **Effects** tabs, and click the one you want to apply.

   The selected filter is added to the **Trial Zone**, and the main window shows a preview of your photo with the filter applied.

2. Experiment with the filter settings in the **Trial Zone**—you can drag the sliders, or enter values directly—to suit your requirements.

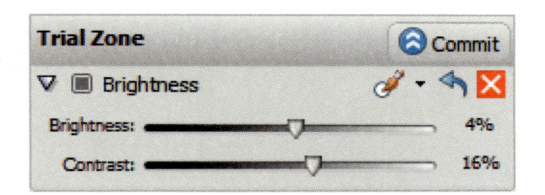

3. (Optional) To replace the trial filter, click a different thumbnail.

> Selecting a new filter always replaces the current filter.

4. To apply the filter, click **Commit** to add it to the **Filters** stack. Repeat to apply additional filters.

5. To apply all filters in the **Filters** stack and close PhotoLab, click **OK**.

Retouching

PhotoLab's main toolbar provides some useful retouching tools. These are commonly used to correct photos before applying colour correction and effects.

- **Red-eye tool**, to remove red eye from a human subject.

- **Spot-repair tool**, to remove blemishes from human skin and material surfaces.

For instructions on using the retouching tools, see DrawPlus Help.

Selective masking

You may sometimes want to apply a filter to selected regions of a photo, rather than to the entire photo. In PhotoLab, you can do this by using a "mask" to define these region(s).

In the example below, a mask has been used to protect the subject of the photo from a **Stained Glass** filter effect.

To apply a mask:

1. On an individual filter, from the ![] **Mask** drop-down list, select **New Mask**.

2. In the pane on the right, select the ![] **Add Region** tool.

3. Adjust the settings to suit your requirements. For example, adjust **Brush Size** to paint larger or more intricate regions.

4. In the **Mode** drop-down list, choose one of the following options:

   - **Select:** Choose this if you want to apply the filter only to the regions you paint. This is the default setting.

   - **Protect:** Choose this if you want to apply the filter to all areas of the photo, except for those that you paint.

5. Using the circular cursor, paint the regions to be masked (selected areas are painted in green; protected areas in red).

   If you've not been as accurate as you'd like while painting, click ![] **Remove Regions** then paint over the unwanted painted regions.

6. Click ![] to save your mask changes.

11 Effects

Using graphic styles

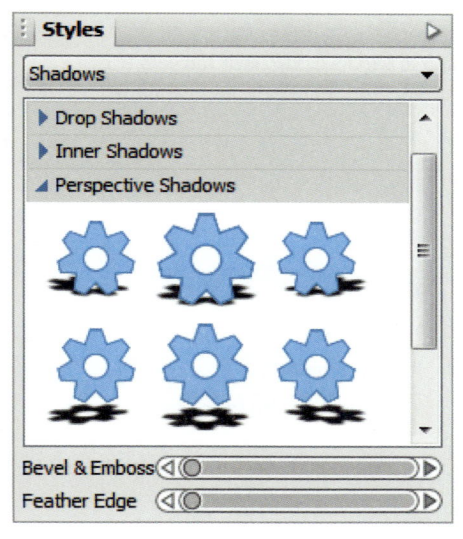

The **Styles tab** contains multiple galleries of pre-designed styles that you can apply to any object, or customize to suit your own taste! Galleries exist in effect categories such as 3D, Bevels, Blurs, Edges, Shadows, and other 2D and 3D filter effects, with each category having further subcategories.

The Styles tab also lets you store your own graphic styles in a **My Styles** section if you would like to reuse them—the style is made available in any DrawPlus drawing. You can add and delete your items within each category, with the option of naming elements to facilitate rapid retrieval.

> You can create your own folders and categories from the Style tab's **Tab Menu** by selecting **Graphic Style Manager** from the menu.

To apply a graphic style to one or more objects:

1. Display the **Styles** tab.

2. Expand the drop-down menu to select a named style category (e.g., Shadows), then pick a subcategory by scrolling the lower window.

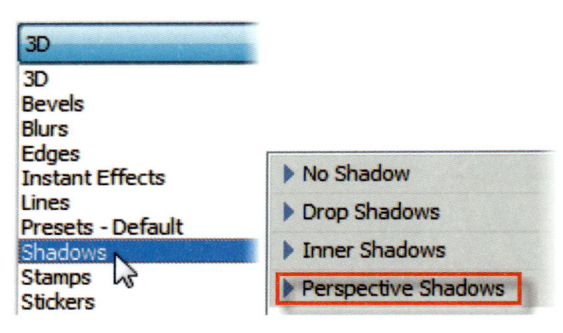

3. Preview available styles as thumbnails (cog shapes are shown by default) in the window.

4. Click a style thumbnail to apply it to the selected object(s).

Saving custom graphic styles

Once you've come up with a set of attributes that you like—properties for fill, line, text, and 2D/3D effects, and so on—you can save this cluster of attributes as a named **graphic style**. DrawPlus saves graphic styles to the Styles tab (My Styles folder by default), which can be subsequently applied to other newly drawn objects.

As each graphic style includes settings for a host of object attributes you can include or exclude certain attributes, making this a powerful tool.

To create a new graphic style based on an existing object's attributes:

1. Select **Create Graphic Styles** from the **Format** menu.

    The Graphic Style Editor dialog appears, with a list of graphic properties and attributes on the left and a four-pane preview region, showing how the graphic style looks on sample objects (Cog, Rounded Rectangle, Sample Text, or the Letter A).

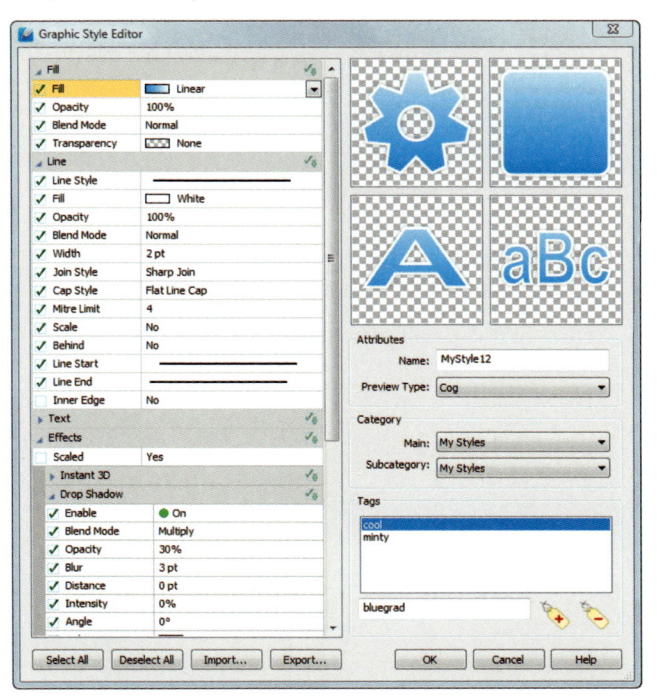

2. (Optional) Click to expand or collapse sections within the list of attributes. This reveals which attributes are currently set. Uncheck any attributes you want to exclude from the style definition, or check any you want to additionally include.

3. (Optional) If you want to modify any attribute, select its value and edit via flyout, drop-down list, dialog, or input box.

4. Type a **Name** to identify the style thumbnail, and optionally, save to a different **Preview Type** (see above) instead of the default cog shape; this preview type will show in the Styles tab.

5. Select the Style tab's **Main** category and **Subcategory** where you want to save the style thumbnail to. Styles are saved to the tab's My Styles category by default. You'll need to create any custom categories in advance.

6. Click **OK**. A thumbnail for the new graphic style appears in the designated Styles tab category.

To create a graphic style from scratch:

1. In the Styles tab, navigate to a category in which you want to create your new style.

2. Click **Add New Graphic Style**.
   - or -

   Right-click any thumbnail and select **Add New Style**.

3. From the dialog, configure attributes via flyout, drop-down list, dialog, or input box.

Applying 2D filter effects

Applying bevels and embossing effects

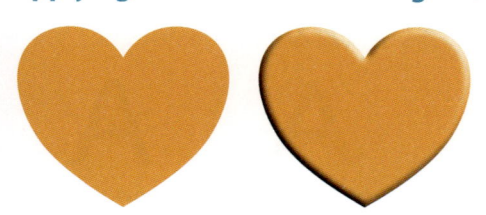

You can apply some depth to your objects by applying an embossing effect.

- From the Styles tab, adjust the **Bevel & Emboss** setting on your selected object. The greater the value, the greater the embossed effect.

Applying feathered edges

Feathering applies a softer edge to your objects, such as embellishments or cut materials. The effect is especially useful for presenting a photo on the page.

- From the Styles tab, pick a **Feather Edge** setting. This is the distance inside the object's outline within which feathering will be applied.

Advanced 2D filter effects

fx For more advanced control of filter effects, a **Filter Effects** dialog can be used to apply filter effects to an object. The following filter effect examples are possible via the dialog. Each effect is shown when applied to the letter "A."

Drop Shadow   **Inner Shadow**   **Outer Glow**   **Inner Glow**

Inner Bevel   **Outer Bevel**   **Emboss**   **Pillow Emboss**

Gaussian Blur   **Zoom Blur**   **Radial Blur**   **Motion Blur**

Colour Fill   **Feather**   **Outline**

To apply 2D filter effects:

1. Click **fx** **Filter Effects** on the **Drawing** toolbar. The Filter Effects dialog appears.

2. To apply a particular effect, check its box in the list at left.

3. To adjust the properties of a specific effect, select its name and vary the dialog controls. Adjust the sliders or enter specific values to vary the combined effect. (You can also select a slider and use the keyboard arrows.) Options differ from one effect to another.

4. Click **OK** to apply the effect or **Cancel** to abandon changes.

Applying 3D filter effects

3D filter effects go beyond 2D filter effects (shadows, bevel, emboss, etc.) to create the impression of a textured surface on the object itself. Keep in mind that none of these 3D effects will "do" anything to an unfilled object—you'll need to have a fill there to see the difference they make!

The Studio's Styles tab is a good place to begin experimenting with 3D filter effects. Its multiple categories each offer a gallery full of predefined effects, using various settings.

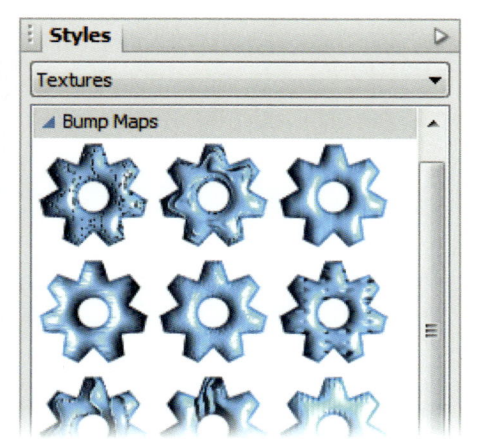

You'll see a variety of remarkable 3D surface (Glass, Metallic, Wood, etc.) and texture presets in the Instant Effects and Textures categories, respectively. Click any thumbnail to apply it to the selected object. Assuming the object has some colour on it to start with, you'll see an instant result!

fx Alternatively, you can customize a preset, or apply one or more specific effects from scratch, by choosing **Filter Effects** from the **Drawing** toolbar. If you want to keep the effect for future, you can save it.

To apply 3D Effects:

1. Choose *fx* **Filter Effects** from the **Drawing** toolbar.
2. Check **3D Effects** in the Filter Effects dialog.
3. Adjust the "master control" sliders here to vary the overall properties of any individual 3D effects you select.

    - **Blur** specifies the amount of smoothing applied (in point size). Larger blur sizes give the impression of broader, more gradual changes in height.
    - **Depth** specifies how steep the changes in depth appear (in point size).
    - The ➕ button is normally down, which links the two sliders so that sharp changes in Depth are smoothed out by the Blur parameter. To adjust the sliders independently, click the button so it's up.

4. Check a 3D effect in the 3D Effects list which reflects the 3D effect you can achieve.

Adding drop shadows

You can apply simple drop shadows by using the **Shadow Tool**. When applied, the selected object is given a sense of depth.

The **Shadow Tool** offers freeform control of the drop shadow effect. With its on-the-page control nodes and supporting Shadow context toolbar, the tool offers various adjustments such as Opacity, Blur, and X (or Y) Shear. Nodes appear on the object for fine control.

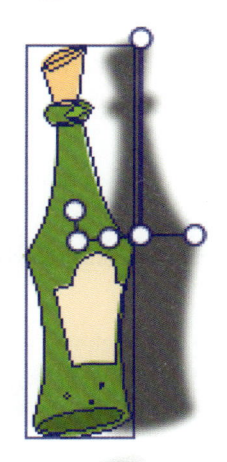

Simple shadow
(drag from object centre)

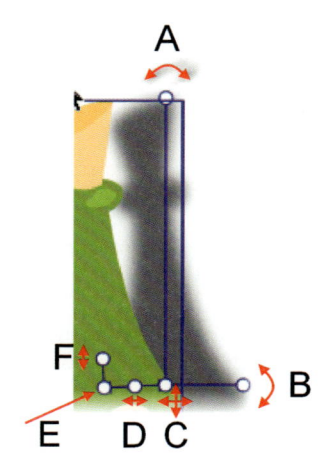

Node controls:
*(**A**) Shear X/Scale Y, (**B**) Shear Y/Scale X,*
*(**C**) Reposition shadow, (**D**) Opacity,*
*(**E**) Lock Point, (**F**) Blur.*
(showing control nodes)

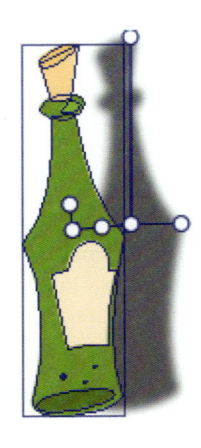

With subtle Shear and Scale adjustments you can produce **skewed shadows** for realistic 2D lighting effects. The example opposite has had adjustments to Shear X and Shear Y, with blurring and reduced opacity.

Applying drop shadows with Shadow Tool

1. Click the **Shadow Tool** on the **Drawing** toolbar. You'll notice control nodes appear which allow adjustment as described in the annotated illustration above.

2. Drag across the object to create a drop shadow (note additional nodes being created).

3. Change blur, opacity, shear, or scale accordingly by node adjustment (or via the displayed context toolbar).

> 💡 If you want to create simple shadows without additional control of the above properties, disable **Advanced** on the context toolbar, then drag the shadow to a new position.

To change a shadow's colour:

- Select a colour from the Studio's Colour tab.

To remove the shadow from an object:

- Double-click the object while the Shadow Tool is selected.

Effects   **155**

Creating blends

Blends enable you to create shapes between two separate shapes on the page. These could be identical in shape but have different line/fill properties or be differently shaped. For the latter, the blending process "morphs" one shape into the other shape.

Each step creates an intermediate shape, where the colour, transparency, and line properties may all change, along with the object shape, during the blend process.

For identical shapes:

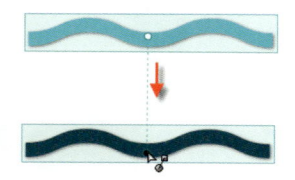

For different shapes (e.g. a blend between a Quick Ellipse and a Quick Petal):

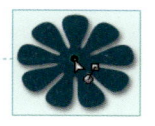

To create a blend with the Blend Tool:

1. Select the **Blend Tool** button on the **Drawing** toolbar.

2. (Optional) From the displayed Context toolbar, choose:

    - The number of "morph" **Blend Steps** to be taken between both points (to increase/decrease the smoothness of the blend).

    - A **Position Profile** or **Attribute Profile** for non-uniform blends—use for rate or transform and blend, respectively.

    - A **Colour Blend Type** which defines how colour distribution occurs between the originating and destination object.

3. Hover over the object to display the Blend cursor.

4. Click and drag the cursor, drawing a dashed line as you go, to your destination point (this must be on an object) and release.

Blending on a path

DrawPlus allows you to make your blended objects conform to a drawn freeform line or curve.

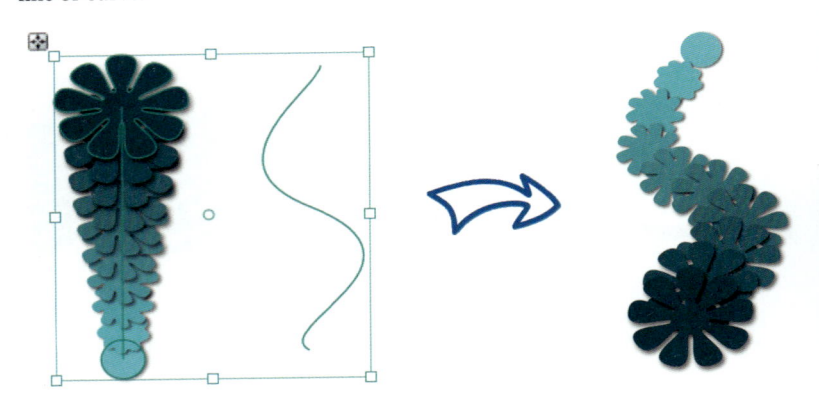

To fit a blend to a line or curve:

1. Select the line or curve and the previously blended object.

2. From the **Tools** menu, select **Fit Blend to Curve**.

Applying perspective

The **Perspective Tool**, like the Envelope Tool, produces an overall shape distortion. Perspective gives you the visual impression of a flat surface being tilted (or skewed) in space, with an exaggerated front/back size differential.

To apply a perspective effect:

1. Select an object and click **Perspective Tool** on the **Drawing** toolbar's Transform flyout. The Node Tool becomes the active tool and an adjustment slider appears above the object.

2. Drag the "3D" cursor over the selected object or drag the special adjustment slider handle left or right to see it respond by tilting in all sorts of orientations. Use Undo if you're not happy with a particular adjustment.
    - or -
    From the context toolbar, select an item from the **Perspective Presets** flyout closest to the effect you're after. The first item, **User Defined perspective**, retrieves the last drawn custom perspective shape used in your current DrawPlus session. You can still use the cursor and handles for adjusting perspective.

Applying envelopes

An envelope distortion is one that you can apply to any object to change its shape without having to edit its nodes. You can use envelopes to bend text into a wave, arch, trapezoid, or just about any other shape. You can edit envelopes into custom shapes and apply them to other objects for corresponding effects.

To apply an envelope:

1. Select the object(s) you want to be enveloped.

2. Click ✉ **Envelope Tool** on the **Drawing** toolbar's Transform flyout.

3. From the context toolbar, select an envelope preset from the **Preset Envelopes** flyout. The first item, User Defined envelope, retrieves the last drawn custom envelope shape used in your current DrawPlus session.

To remove an envelope:

- Select the envelope with the **Envelope Tool**, then choose ⊗ **Remove Envelope** from the Envelope context toolbar.

To create/edit your own envelope:

1. Select the object(s) with the **Envelope Tool**.

2. Drag the nodes and handles accordingly.

Using stencils

The **Stencils** tab provides a selection of ready-to-go, fun stencils that will add impact to any page. Whether you paint over them with the **Brush Tool**, or use them to cut out a design from a picture, stencils provide endless opportunities for creativity.

If you're feeling really creative, you can create your own stencils by dragging objects to the **Stencils** tab.

Adding stencils to your page

1. On the **Stencils** tab, click the drop-down list to select a category.

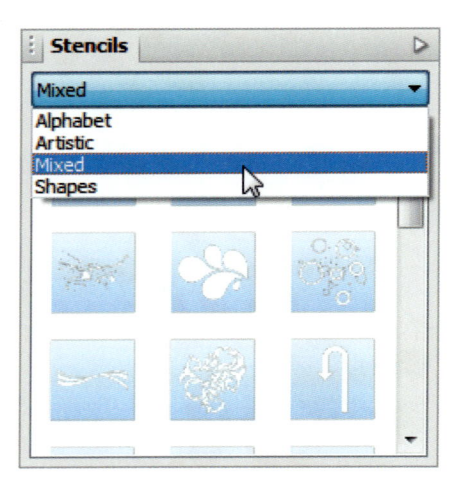

   The lower gallery displays thumbnails of the stencils available in the selected category.

2. Click and drag a thumbnail from the gallery onto your page.

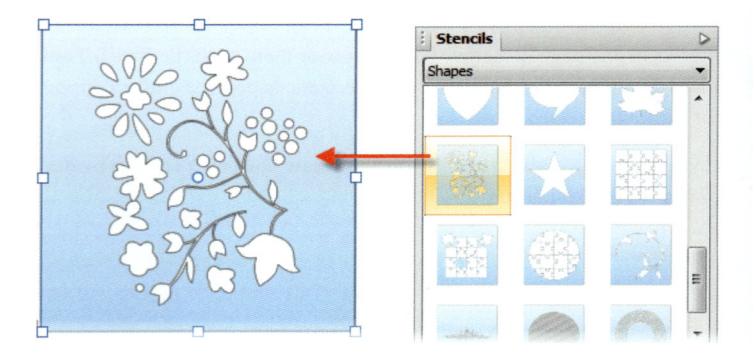

Painting over stencils

1. Add a stencil to your page.

2. From the **Drawing** toolbar, click the **Brush Tool**.

3. Choose a brush type from the **Brushes** tab and set your brush colour on the Colour tab. (See Applying brush strokes on p. 63.)

> Brushes in the **Effects**, **Paint** and **Spray** categories are particularly suited to stencil work.

4. Paint over the stencil with your chosen brush.

   Swap to different brush colours or brush types using respective Colour and Brushes tabs.

5. From the **Drawing** toolbar, select the **Pointer Tool**.

6. Click the stencil, then select **Lift Stencil** below the stencil. The stencil is removed, revealing the painted design beneath it.

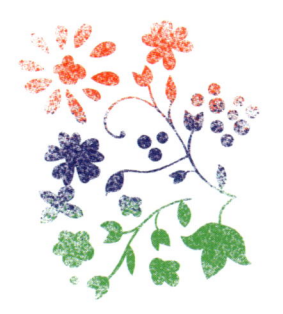

12 Stopframe/Keyframe Animation

Getting started with animation

What is animation? Like flip books, cartoon movies and TV, it's a way of creating the illusion of motion by displaying a series of still images, rapidly enough to fool the eye—or more accurately, the brain. Professional animators have developed a whole arsenal of techniques for character animation—rendering human (and animal) movement in a convincing way.

A clear distinction has to be made between two types of animation techniques, both possible from within DrawPlus, i.e.

- **Stopframe animation**: also known as Stop motion animation, involves the animation of static objects frame-by-frame. In the film industry, Stopframe animation is used within widely known productions based on figures made of clay or other bendable material.

- **Keyframe animation**: performs movement of computer-generated objects from basic shapes to cartoon characters (used traditionally in Stopframe animation). Using the power of computing, smooth playback of animated objects is easily achieved between key moments in your animation, defined by the user as **Keyframes**.

DrawPlus lets you export Stopframe or Keyframe animations to a variety of different formats. For more details, review Exporting animations (see p. 180). For now we'll look at how to set up both Stopframe and Keyframe animations.

To begin a new Stopframe or Keyframe animation (from Startup Wizard):

1. Start DrawPlus (or choose **File>New>New from Startup Wizard** if it's already running).

2. Select **Create>Stopframe Animation** or **Create>Keyframe Animation** from the Startup Wizard.

3. From **Page Setup**, review document types in the left-hand pane.

4. Select a document type thumbnail from a category in the left-hand pane.

5. (Optional) For custom settings, from the right-hand of the dialog, click a **Paper** or **Animation** properties setting and either choose a different drop-down list option or input new values to modify. Typically, you can change Width, Height, and Orientation settings in the **Paper** category.

6. Click **OK**. The new document opens.

To begin a new Stopframe or Keyframe animation from scratch:

- Either:

    - Select **New>New Stopframe Animation** from the **File** menu.
      - or -

    - Select **New>New Keyframe Animation** from the **File** menu.

A new document window opens in the respective Animation mode.

> 💡 You can convert any drawing into either animation type from the **File** Menu.
>
> 💡 Modify Page Setup such as page size and orientation from the Pages context toolbar.

To save an animation:

- Choose **File>Save** DrawPlus saves animation documents in the proprietary .dpa format.

Working with Stopframe animation

In Stopframe animation mode you'll be working predominantly with the Frames tab. It is ideally suited for animation because of its width and easy control of individual frames (stopframes are spread along the tab for easier management).

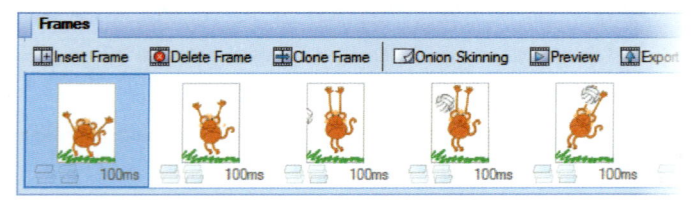

To view the Frames tab:

- Unless the tab is already displayed, click the ▬▲▬ handle at the bottom of your workspace to reveal the tab.

To clone the current frame to a new frame:

- Select a frame in the Frames tab, and choose **Clone Frame**.

The frame is added after the selected frame.

To generate a new blank frame:

- Choose ▦ **Insert Frame** from the Frames tab.

To navigate between frames:

- Click on any visible frame to display its objects on screen (objects can then be edited).

To rename a frame:

- Right-click a frame and choose **Properties**. In the **Name** field, type in a new frame name. The new name is shown on the Hintline toolbar.

To change frame sequence:

- Drag the selected frame to a new position in the frame order. When the dragged frame's thumbnail creates a slightly wider space between two frames than usual, release the mouse button to place the frame to be moved.

To delete a selected frame:

- Click ▦ **Delete Frame** from the Frames tab.

Onion Skinning

Onion skinning is a standard animation technique derived from cel animation, where transparent sheets enable the artist to see through to the preceding frame(s). It's useful for enabling precise registration and controlling object movement from frame to frame.

To turn onion skinning on or off:

1. From the Frames tab, click the ▦ **Onion Skinning** button to turn onion skinning on or off.

2. (Optional) ▦ To set more than one previous frame to be visible, click **Properties**, then set the number of frames in the **Onion Skinning** input box.

The preceding frame's objects will show behind those of the currently selected frame.

Previewing Stopframe animations

You can **preview** your animation prior to export at any time either directly from your Frames tab (shown in a Preview window) or from within your default web browser.

To preview in the Preview window:

- Click **Preview** on the Frames tab.

The animation loads into the Preview window and begins playing at its actual size and speed. You can use the control buttons (Play, Stop, etc.) to review individual frames.

To preview in a web browser:

- Select **Preview in Browser** from the **File** menu. The animation loads your default web browser and begins playing.

Working with Keyframe animation

When compared with Stopframe animation (see Getting started with animation on p. 165), **Keyframe animation** offers a more powerful and efficient animation technology—it saves having to declare every frame, letting your computer do the hard work!

Essentially, the technique lets you create only user-defined **keyframes** through which objects animate, with each keyframe containing **Key objects** which can be assigned a position, rotation, attributes, etc.

Intermediate steps between Key objects are created automatically and produce a smooth professional-looking inter-object transition (this is called **Tweening**); Tweened objects are created as a result.

The Storyboard tab is the workspace for laying out your animation "story" in a chronological keyframe-by-keyframe sequence (from left to right).

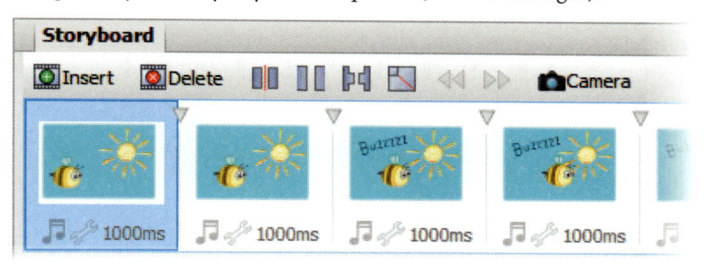

On export, your animation will play in this direction. Using the above "bee" animation in the tab illustration as an example, the bee is animated, while the sun and "Buzzzz" text remain static objects.

By adding objects (bee and sun) to a starting keyframe it's possible to automatically copy (or more correctly **run forward**) those objects forward when you create subsequent keyframes. This in itself doesn't affect animation, but it's the repositioning of a run forward object (such as the bee) in later keyframes that creates "movement."

Once keyframes are created, the animator has a great deal of control over how objects are run forward (or even backwards). You can introduce objects anywhere on the storyboard (so they appear for a limited time), and either run them forward or backwards by a specific number of keyframes (or right to the start or end of the storyboard). The "Buzzzz" text in the above example will only show from keyframes 3 onwards.

Supporting tabs

Keyframe animation mode also presents other tabs that support the Storyboard tab. These are exclusively used within keyframe animation (and do not show in normal or stopframe animation mode), i.e.

- The **Easing tab** is used for applying linear or non-linear changes between key objects with use of editable envelopes (e.g., to change object position, morph, scale, rotation, skew, colour, and transparency).

- The **Actions tab** allows objects and keyframes to be attributed actions which will run (e.g., go to a URL or designated marker) when an event is triggered (e.g., MouseOver, Rollovers, etc.).

A keyframe camera, masking, and sound/movies can also be used in keyframe animation.

See DrawPlus Help for more information.

Getting started

To create a keyframe animation:

1. Select **Create>Keyframe Animation** on the Startup Wizard.
2. From **Page Setup**, review document types in the left-hand pane.
3. Select a document type thumbnail from a Web, Screen, or Mobile category in the left-hand pane—ideal for presentation via website (banners, adverts, etc.), as a computer presentation, or on a handheld device.
4. (Optional) In the **Paper** section at the right-hand of the dialog, swap your measurement units (e.g. to pixels), and change page size and/or orientation.
5. (Optional) In the lower **Animation** section, you can configure animation-specific settings.
6. Click **OK**.

To view the Storyboard tab:

- Unless the tab is already displayed, click the ▬▲▬ handle at the bottom of your workspace to reveal the tab.

We'll assume that you've drawn objects on the first keyframe. You can run forward these automatically throughout your animation by creation of additional keyframes—this builds up your animation "story" quickly. Other methods exist to run objects forward (and backwards) but let's concentrate on the insertion of keyframes to do this.

To insert keyframes:

1. From the Storyboard tab, select a keyframe and choose **Insert**.
2. From the dialog, choose the **Number of keyframes** to add to the Storyboard tab. Set a default **Keyframe duration** for each created keyframe.
3. Choose to add keyframe(s) at a **Location** before or after the currently selected keyframe or before/after the first or last keyframe.
4. (Optional) Check **Insert blank keyframes** if you don't want to include run forward objects in your keyframes. Blank frames are useful "filler" frames that add breaks in your animation for messages, logos, etc.
5. Click **OK**.

To view or edit a particular keyframe:

- Select a keyframe in the Storyboard tab.

To delete a keyframe:

- Select the keyframe and choose **Delete**.

Keyframe duration

Keyframe duration represents the amount of time in between each individual keyframe.

To set the duration of an individual keyframe:

- Click the keyframe's duration (e.g., 1500ms) under its thumbnail, and, when selected, type a new value then click away.

> The total duration of your animation is shown on your last keyframe, e.g. (5.0s).

Adding sound

To complement the visual effect of your keyframe animation it's possible to add audio. Sounds can be added either for the duration of a specific keyframe, or when an action is applied to an object event (see DrawPlus Help for details on actions and events).

To add an audio clip:

1. On the Storyboard tab, click on the keyframe's **Sound** icon (located below the frame's thumbnail).
2. From the dialog, navigate to your audio file, select it and click the **Open** button.

To remove a selected keyframe's audio clip, right-click and select **Clear Background Sound**.

Adding movies

As well as using sound in your keyframe animation, you can introduce movie clips via **Insert>Movie Clip**. The movie is inserted into your chosen keyframe as an object which like any other object (QuickShape, Text, etc.) will need to be run forward for the movie to play throughout the animation.

DrawPlus supports various video formats including Flash Video (FLV), Flash SWF, AVI, WMV, and QuickTime.

Previewing keyframe animations

From the Storyboard tab, you can **preview** your animation at any time either in a web browser or in Flash Player (This is a DrawPlus install option). This is a quick way of checking it prior to export.

Keyframe object control

A whole series of important **object control** tools are also available in keyframe animation. They are available on an **object toolbar**, displayed in-context under any selected object.

Initial grouped objects show run forward, and grouped object buttons

Objects along the animation run show buttons for conversion to key objects, and object placement and attributes buttons in both directions.

The insertion of keyframes when you begin your animation will automatically run objects forward or backward. However, **Run Forward** and **Run Backward** commands let you introduce new objects in your animation which run across a limited number of keyframes or the entire storyboard.

174 Stopframe/Keyframe Animation

To run object(s) forward/backward:

1. Select the keyframe which contains your chosen object.

2. Select the object, then click ▶▶ **Run forward** (or ◀◀ **Run backward** if on a later keyframe), located on the object toolbar directly under the selected object.

3. From the dialog, choose to **Run Length** either **To end of storyboard** or by **N Keyframes** (enter a number of keyframes to copy to).

Once run forward or backward, you can move an object on any keyframe (normally the last) to make animation work. Objects that are not moved are called **tweened objects**, and show as transparent square nodes (see below; **B**) which are automatically created between any two **key objects** (**A**). If you move any of these interim tweened objects you change your animation to follow a non-linear path (see below)—as a result, the tweened object becomes a key object (**C**).

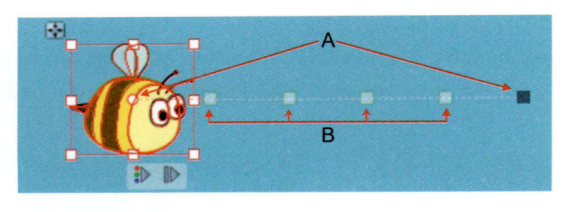

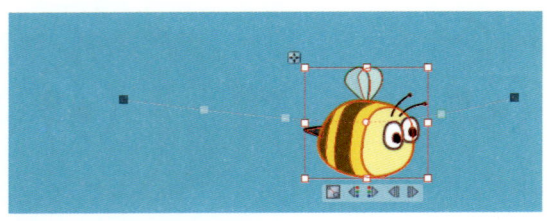

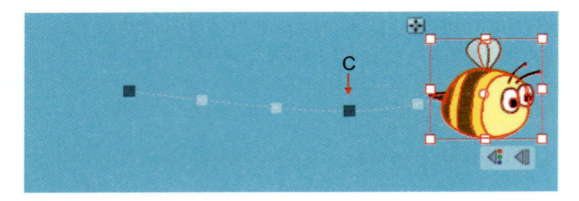

This takes care of repositioning objects, but what about changing an object's transform (morph, scale, rotation, and shear) or attribute (colour or transparency)? Simply, a selected tweened object can be modified just like any other object—it will be converted to a key object automatically as a transform or attribute change is applied.

> Use **Convert to key object** to lock a tweened object into place (by making it a key object). Use the opposite command, **Convert to tweened object**, to convert back to a tweened object (removing any repositioning, transforms, or attributes local to the object). Both options are on the object toolbar.

The Object toolbar also offers two commands for repositioning objects along the storyboard. **Update placement backward** updates a previous object's position to match the selected key or tweened object's current position. Conversely, **Update placement forward** updates later object's position accordingly.

Like DrawPlus's Format Painter, you can also apply a specific object's attributes (colour, transparency, filter effects, shadows, etc.) to previous or later objects with **Update attributes backward** or **Update attributes forward**.

Autorun

Although switched off by default, this advanced feature speeds up the animation process by automatically creating objects, their placement and attributes along the length of the storyboard, from a specific keyframe onwards. Even when editing an object, the changes are reflected throughout. Without Autorun enabled, objects are presented across keyframes by using the Insert button or clicking the object toolbar's **Run forward** or **Run backward** buttons.

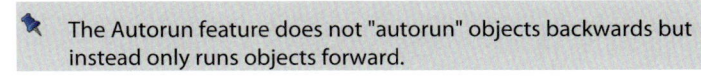

> The Autorun feature does not "autorun" objects backwards but instead only runs objects forward.

To autorun objects:

1. Click **Autorun** on the Storyboard tab. The button is highlighted when enabled. Click again to disable.

2. Create or modify an object on a keyframe to see the effect on the object in subsequent keyframes.

176 Stopframe/Keyframe Animation

Joints

In both Stopframe and Keyframe animation, the ability to simulate movement about a fixed point is the basis for the natural movement of animated characters.

In DrawPlus animation modes, the **Joint Tool** can be used to create natural movement by rotating objects about a joint that connects two separate objects. By cloning stopframes or running forward keyframes, the objects, once rotated about a shared joint, will animate.

To visualize this, think of a wooden artist's dummy or a dancing puppet (below) which can be moved into different positions by rotating about individual or multiple joints.

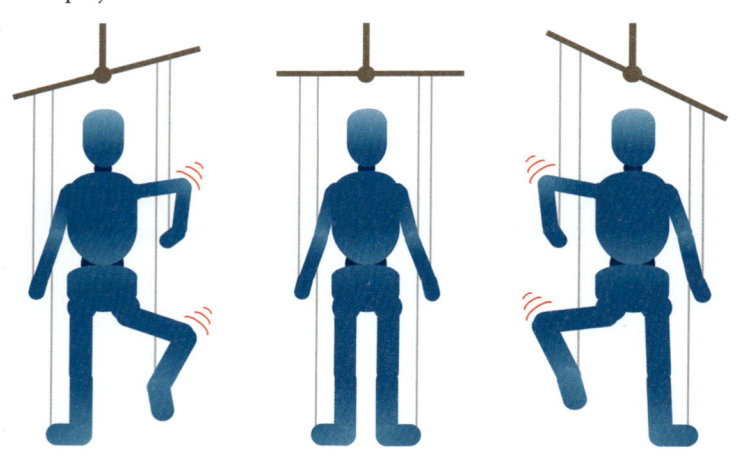

Creating joints

To create a joint:

1. Draw a collection of objects that you plan to connect together.

2. Select the **Joint Tool** on the **Drawing** toolbar's Selection flyout.

3. Select the object you want to add a joint to.

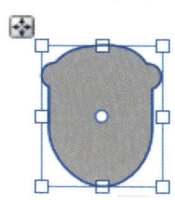

4. From the Joint context toolbar, select **Add Joint**.

5. Position the cursor on the selected object where you want to add your joint.

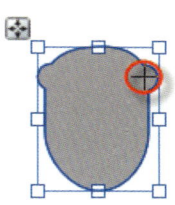

6. Click to add your joint, which will show as a white circular node.

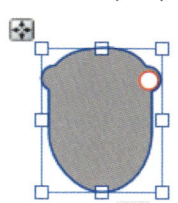

7. Repeat for other objects.

> Before connecting objects together, a joint must be present on each object to allow both to be joined together.

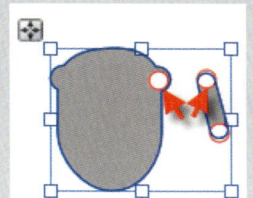

To delete a joint:

1. With the Joint Tool enabled, select the object with the joint attached.

2. From the Joint context toolbar, select **Delete Joint**.

3. Position the cursor over the joint and click.

Connecting joints

Like a snap-together toy, objects with joints can be snapped together joint-to-joint. In doing so, objects become connected and can then pivot about the shared joint.

To connect two joints together:

1. With the Joint Tool enabled, drag one object over the other object, so that the joints overlap. The node will turn from white to green (on hover over), then black (on mouse button release).

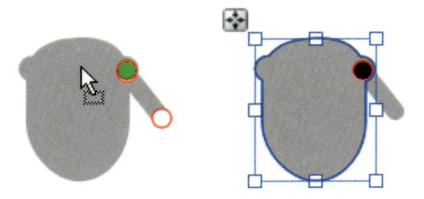

2. Repeat for other objects.

To disconnect objects:

- With the Joint Tool enabled, drag a connected object away from the other object.

> Green joints always indicate that the objects can be joined; black joints indicate that the objects are already connected at that joint.
>
> Press the **Esc** key to cancel the operation.

Stopframe/Keyframe Animation **179**

Animating objects with joints

Once you've created your jointed objects, you'll want to animate them. For Keyframe animation, you can rotate your object about its joints on specific keyframes just as for any other rotation operation. Similarly, for Stopframe animation, individual frames can be cloned, then objects rotated about their joints.

> For successful animation, always use the Joint Tool for joint rotations. Use of the Pointer Tool and Rotate Tool should be avoided.

To rotate jointed objects:

- With the Joint Tool enabled, create a marquee selection (i.e., drag your cursor) over the joint(s) that you wish to rotate. For example, for an arm, drag over the wrist (A), (B) wrist+elbow, or (C) wrist+elbow+shoulder to rotate by the wrist, elbow or shoulder, respectively.

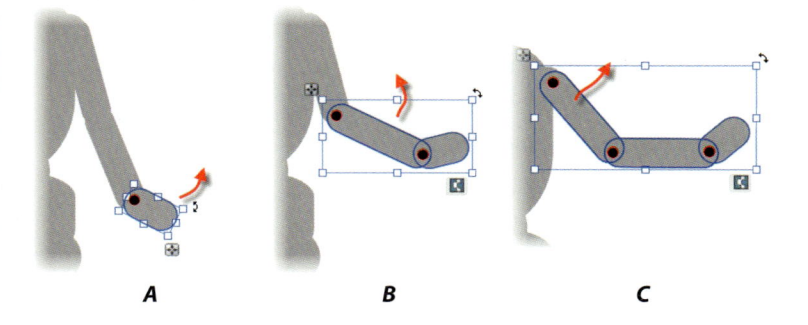

A *B* *C*

> Objects with more than two joints cannot be rotated.

> If you're not using animation, joints can still be used to simulate motion on drawings.

Exporting animations

Exporting your stopframe or keyframe animation outputs your animation to a file which can be shared or viewed, either standalone or when included as part of a web page. DrawPlus lets you export to a variety of formats as indicated below:

Export	Stopframe	Keyframe
Flash SWF	✘	✓
Flash Lite/i-Mode	✘	✓
Video	✓	✓
Image	✓	✓

To export your animation as a Flash file:

1. Choose **Export>Export as Flash SWF** from the **File** menu.

2. From the dialog, provide a ShockWave Flash file name and folder location, and click the **Save** button. You'll see an export progress dialog appear until the Flash file is created.

To export to Flash Lite/i-Mode:

1. Choose **Export>Export as Flash Lite/i-Mode** from the **File** menu.

2. From the dialog, provide a ShockWave Flash file name and folder location, and click the **Save** button. You'll see an export progress dialog appear until the file is created.

To export animation as video:

1. Choose **Export>Export As Video** from the **File** menu.

2. From the displayed dialog's Basic tab, select your chosen export type from the **File type** and **Template** drop-down list according to the type of output video format you require.

3. (Optional) Click **Match project settings** to set an approximate video frame size based on your animation project's Page size (set in Page Setup).

4. Specify a name for file in the **Filename** box, clicking **Browse** and selecting a new location if you first wish to choose an alternate drive or folder to store your file.

5. (Optional) Set an export **Quality**.

6. Click the **Export** button. Your project will then be composed and converted into the specified format and you will be shown a progress bar during this process.

> Keyframe animations exported as video do not support audio.

Within Stopframe animation, this option lets you create an animated GIF by default, which we'll focus on here. For keyframe animation, you can export a single keyframe as any type of image format.

To export as an animated GIF:

1. Choose **Export** from the Frames tab.

2. Click the **Export** button (or **Close** to simply record the settings if you plan to preview in a browser first).

3. Provide a file name and folder location, and click **Save**. Don't worry if you have extra white space around your image. Any unused border area will be cropped automatically, just as you saw in the Preview window.

13 Publishing and Exporting

Interactive Print/PDF Preview

The **Print/PDF Preview** mode changes the screen view to display your layout without frames, guides, rulers, and other screen items. Supporting toolbars allow for a comprehensive and interactive preview of your pages before printing or publishing as PDF.

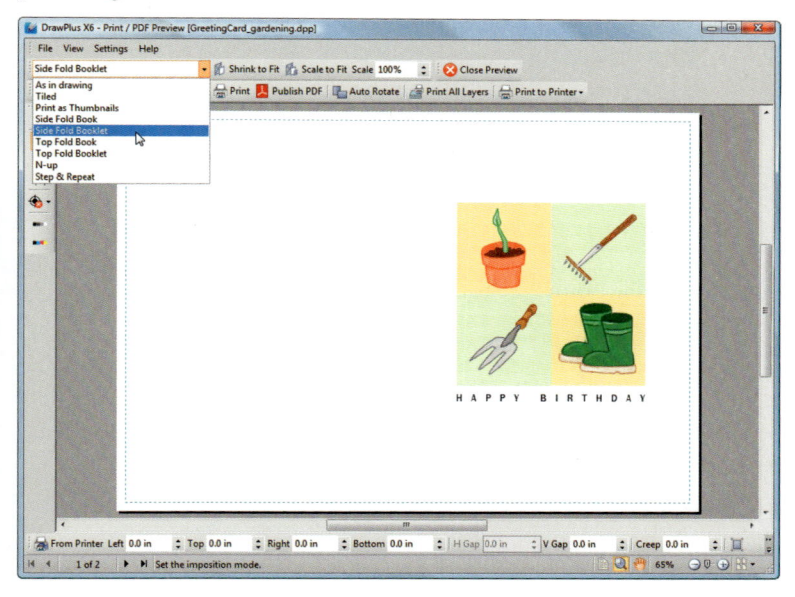

Print Preview is interactive because a main feature is to provide **print-time imposition**. Put simply, this allows you to create folded books, booklets, and more, **at the printing stage** from unfolded basic page setups. Other interactive features are also available while in Preview mode.

- Select installed printers, and choose which pages to print and how they print (to printer, file or separation).
- Add and adjust printer margins.
- Switch on/off page marks when generating professional output.

To preview the printed page:

1. From the **File** menu, select **Print/PDF Preview**.

    In Print/PDF Preview, your first printer sheet is displayed according to your printer's setup.

2. (Optional) Choose an installed printer from the **Printer** toolbar's drop-down list.
3. (Optional) Adjust printer margins from the **Margins** toolbar.
4. Review your design using the page navigation controls at the bottom of your workspace.

To print:

- From the **Printer** toolbar, select **Print**.
  - or -

    From the **File** menu, select **Print**.

The standard Print dialog is then displayed, where settings are carried over from Preview mode.

To publish as PDF:

- From the **Printer** toolbar, select **Publish PDF**.
  - or -

    From the **File** menu, select **Publish PDF**.

The standard **Publish PDF** dialog is then displayed.

To cancel Print Preview mode:

- Select **Close Preview** from the top of your workspace (or click the window's **Close** button).

Print-time imposition

During preview, you can enable imposition of your drawing, choosing a mode suited to your intended final drawing (book, booklet, etc.). Each mode displays different toolbar options on the context-sensitive **Imposition** toolbar. Document imposition is not limited to desktop printing—it can also be used when creating a press-ready PDF for professional printing.

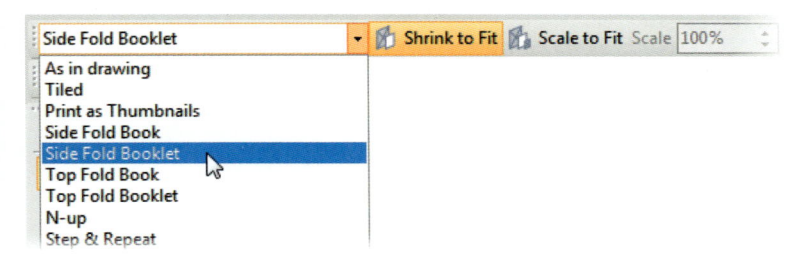

To choose an imposition mode:

- From the **Imposition** toolbar, select an option from the **Imposition Mode** drop-down list.

Printing basics

DrawPlus supports printing directly to a physical desktop printer (e.g., All-in-ones, Inkjet and Laser printers) or to an electronic file such as Adobe Acrobat PDF (see p. 189). Printing your document to a desktop printer is one of the more likely operations you'll be performing in DrawPlus. The easy-to-use Print dialog presents the most commonly used options to you, with a navigable "live" Preview window to check your print output.

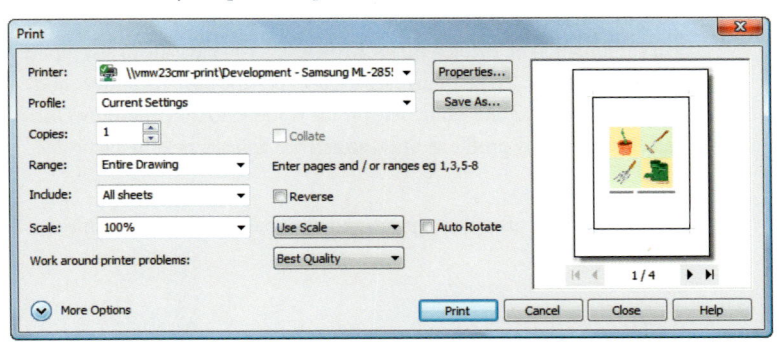

The dialog also supports additional printing options via the **More Options** button including **Double-sided Printing**, **Manual Duplex**, and many other useful printing options. One particular option, called **Layout**, allows for print-time imposition of your document—simply create a booklet or other folded document at the print stage.

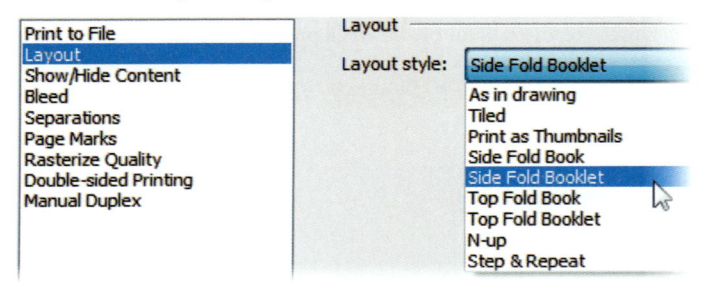

Print to File	Layout
Layout	Layout style: **Side Fold Booklet**
Show/Hide Content	As in drawing
Bleed	Tiled
Separations	Print as Thumbnails
Page Marks	Side Fold Book
Rasterize Quality	**Side Fold Booklet**
Double-sided Printing	Top Fold Book
Manual Duplex	Top Fold Booklet
	N-up
	Step & Repeat

For a detailed description of each option, see Interactive Print/PDF Preview in DrawPlus Help.

> If you're working with a service bureau or commercial printer and need to provide PDF output, see Publishing as PDF on p. 189.

To set up your printer or begin printing:

1. Click **Print** on the **Standard** toolbar. The Print dialog appears.

2. Select a currently installed printer from the **Printer** drop-down list. If necessary, click the **Properties** button to set up the printer for the correct page size, etc.

3. Select a print profile from the **Profile** drop-down list. You can just use **Current Settings** or choose a previously saved custom profile (.ppr) based on a combination of dialog settings; **Browse** lets you navigate to any .ppr file on your computer. To save current settings, click the **Save As** button, and provide a unique profile name. The profile is added to the drop-down list. Note: If you modify profile settings, an asterisk appears next to the profile name.

4. Select the number of copies to print, and optionally instruct the printer to **Collate** them.

5. Select the print **Range** to be printed, e.g. the Entire Drawing, Current Page, or range of pages. For specific pages or a range of pages, enter "1,3,5" or "2-5", or enter any combination of the two.

   To print selected text or objects, make your selection first, then choose Current Selection appearing in the **Range** drop-down list **after selection**.

   Whichever option you've chosen, the **Include** drop-down list lets you export all sheets in the range, or just odd or even sheets, with the option of printing in **Reverse** order.

6. Set a percentage **Scale** which will enlarge or shrink your print output (both page and contents). A 100% scale factor creates a full size print output. Alternatively, from the adjacent drop-down list, choose **Shrink to Fit** to reduce your document's page size to the printer sheet size or **Scale to Fit** to enlarge or reduce the document page size as required.

7. Keep **Auto Rotate** checked if you want your document page to automatically rotate your printer's currently set sheet orientation. When you access the Print dialog, if page and sheet sizes do not match, you'll be prompted to adjust your printer sheet orientation automatically (or you can just ignore auto-rotation).

8. Click **Print**.

Publishing as PDF

DrawPlus can output your drawings to Adobe PDF, ideal for both **screen-ready** distribution and **professional** printing. In DrawPlus, ready-to-go PDF profiles are available for both uses, making PDF setup less complicated.

> DrawPlus lets you operate in a CMYK colour space from document setup to professional PDF output. This involves starting with a new drawing using a CMYK Primary colour space (p. 14), designing using CMYK colours, and publishing a PDF-X1a-compliant PDF file (using the PDF/X-1a printer profile).

To export your document as a PDF file (using a profile):

1. Choose **Publish as PDF** from the **File** menu.

2. Select a profile for screen-ready or professional output from the **Profile** drop-down list.

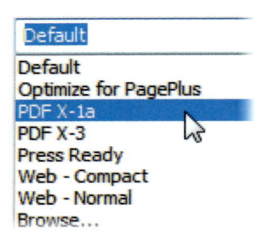

   ```
   Default
   Default
   Optimize for PagePlus
   PDF X-1a
   PDF X-3
   Press Ready
   Web - Compact
   Web - Normal
   Browse...
   ```

   The dialog updates with the selected profile's new settings. The Compatibility is set according to the profile and doesn't need to be set.

3. Select the **Range** to be published, e.g. the Entire Drawing, Current Page, or range of pages. For specific pages or a range of pages, enter "1,3,5" or "2-5", or enter any combination of the two.

   Whichever option you've chosen, the **Include** drop-down list lets you export all sheets in the range, or just odd or even sheets.

4. Set a percentage **Scale** which will enlarge or shrink your published output (both page and contents). A 100% scale factor creates a full size print output.

5. (Optional) Click **More Options** and make any additional settings as required.

6. Click **OK**.

Saving PDF profiles

To save any current combination of your own PDF output settings as a custom publish profile with a unique name, click the **Save As** button next to the Publish profile list. Type in a new name and click OK. In a subsequent session you can recall the profile by selecting its name from the list.

More PDF options

The dialog also supports additional PDF publishing options via the **More Options** button including **Layout**, **Prepress**, and **Colour Management**.

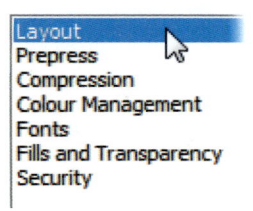

Layout
Prepress
Compression
Colour Management
Fonts
Fills and Transparency
Security

Exporting objects and drawings

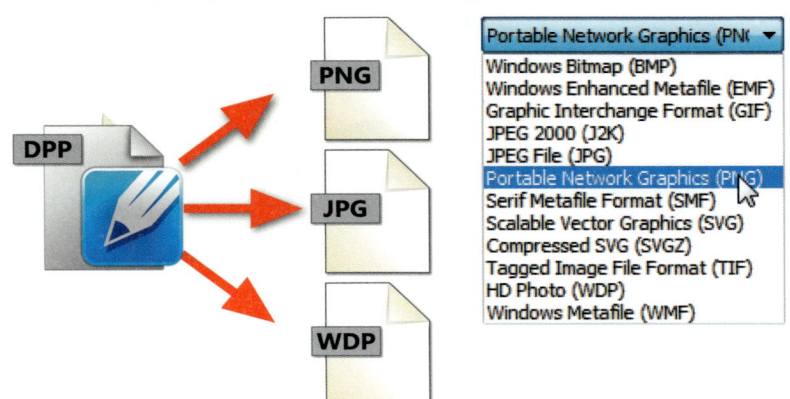

Portable Network Graphics (PN(
Windows Bitmap (BMP)
Windows Enhanced Metafile (EMF)
Graphic Interchange Format (GIF)
JPEG 2000 (J2K)
JPEG File (JPG)
Portable Network Graphics (PNG)
Serif Metafile Format (SMF)
Scalable Vector Graphics (SVG)
Compressed SVG (SVGZ)
Tagged Image File Format (TIF)
HD Photo (WDP)
Windows Metafile (WMF)

You can export at any time by using **Export as Picture** or **Dynamic Preview**; the former lets you compare export settings, the latter allows editing during preview—great for pixel-accurate editing of your intended output!

Exporting as picture

Especially if you're exporting graphics for the web, you can take advantage of the **Picture Export** dialog, which will greatly help you in reducing file sizes and download times as far as possible while maintaining image quality. The dialog lets you export the individual page, all pages, just a selected object(s), or a user-defined region. You can also see how your picture will look (and how much space it will take up) before you save it! For visual comparison, its multi-window display provides side-by-side WYSIWYG previews to compare different formats, or the same format at differing bit depths.

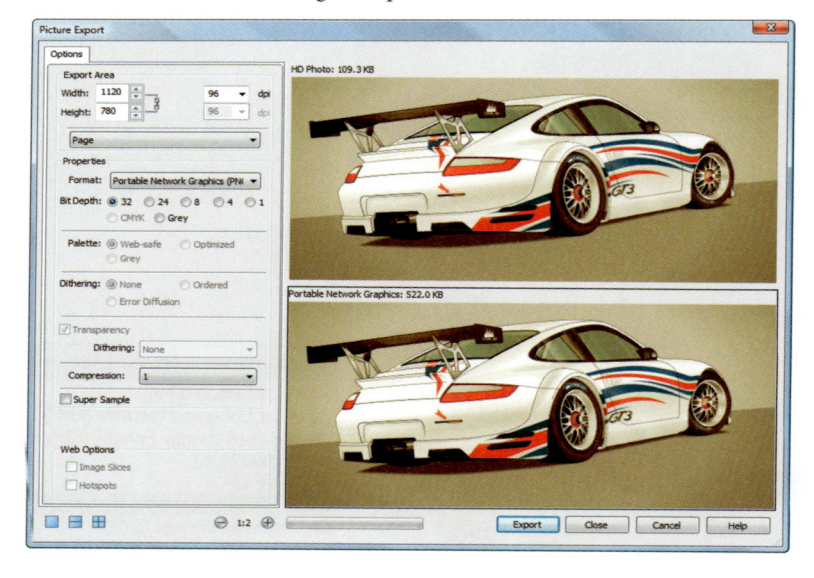

To export as a picture:

1. Choose **Export>Export as Picture** from the **File** menu.

2. (Optional) From the Export Area section, you can scale the picture to a new size if desired (change **Width** and **Height**), or adjust the **dpi** (dots per inch) setting. For graphics to be used on-screen, it's best to leave these values intact.

3. From the drop-down list, choose if the export can be based on the whole **Page**, **All Pages**, **Selected Area**, or **Selected Objects**.

4. From the Properties section, select the intended graphics file format from the **Format** drop-down list. The remaining box area will display different options depending on your chosen graphics format. Change settings as appropriate to the file format selected (see DrawPlus Help for more information).

5. (Optional) From the Web Options section, you can control web elements in your picture, i.e. you can check **Image Slices** or **Hotspots** if you've create these elements and want them exported.

6. Click **Export**. If you click **Close**, DrawPlus remembers your preferred format and settings.

7. From the Export dialog, navigate to a folder of your choice, enter a File name, then click **Save**.

> When exporting Stopframe animations, an Animation tab is shown in the dialog for frame export control.

> For converting DrawPlus objects into pictures on the page, use **Tools>Convert to Picture**.

Defining a region for export

DrawPlus lets you export a specific region in your design. The region, shown as a bounding box, is actually a layer **overlay** which can be resized, repositioned over the export area and shown/hidden. The Picture Export dialog is used for the actual export process.

To define an export region:

1. From the **Standard** toolbar, click **Overlays** and select **Export Overlay** from the drop-down list. A bounding box is overlaid over your page.

2. Drag a corner (or edge) handle to resize the box; reposition the box over the export area.

3. (Optional) Name the Export Overlay layer in the **Export Name** box on the context toolbar (this labels the export overlay in the Layers tab and provides the default file name at export).

- Click **Export** shown under the box. The Picture Export dialog is displayed, from which you can modify and choose an export file format (described previously).

When the overlay is applied, the bounding box is automatically selected (it shows the selection colour of the overlay layer). Clicking away from the box will deselect it (showing the box Colour), but it can be reselected at any time (e.g., for repositioning).

To select the box:

- From the Standard toolbar, select Overlays and then Export Overlay.

Exporting multiple pages

If you have multiple pages in your drawing, you can export any currently viewed page or all pages.

To export the current page:

- From the Pages tab, select a page you wish to export. When you export, the Picture Export dialog will default to export the page, unless objects on the page are selected.

To export all pages:

- From the Picture Export dialog, select **All Pages** in the drop-down list.

For example, exporting a four-page project called mydesign.dpp will create four files called mydesign00.png, mydesign01.png, mydesign02.png, and mydesign03.png.

Exporting as CMYK TIFF or JPEG

For professional printing, you can create a drawing in a CMYK colour space (p. 14), which offers colour predictability during design, processing, and output. You can either publish your design as a PDF document (p. 189) or export as picture, with both options maintaining a CMYK colour space.

To export as a CMYK TIFF or JPEG picture:

- In the Picture Export dialog, enable **CMYK**.

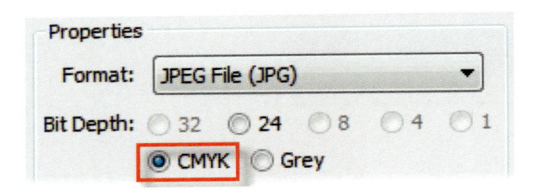

Dynamic preview

Although the Picture Export dialog's preview options lets you see how your export will look, it's time-consuming to repeatedly export your graphic until you get the output exactly as you want it. Instead, you can use **Dynamic Preview**, which lets you swap to a **preview-and-edit** mode, showing how your graphics will export directly on the page. It also lets you edit that output while still previewing, and set up the exported file's name, format and other settings. The ability to fine-tune object positioning to pixel level, aided by a pixel grid (automatically showing at higher page magnification), is beneficial to web graphics developers.

To change export settings:

1. From the **Hintline** toolbar, click the **Dynamic Preview** down arrow and choose **Preview Settings**. The option launches the Dynamic Preview Options dialog, which closely resembles the Picture Export dialog (see above).

2. (Optional) From the Export Area section, scale the picture to a new size if desired (change **pixels**), or adjust the **dpi** (dots per inch) setting.

3. Change settings in the Properties box according to your chosen **Format**. Settings change according to file type (see DrawPlus Help for more information).

4. Click **OK**.

To export via Dynamic Preview:

1. From the **Hintline** toolbar, click the **Dynamic Preview** down arrow and choose **Export Preview As**.

2. From the dialog, you'll be prompted for a file name to which you can save your graphic. Choose a folder location and enter a file name.

To toggle between Normal and Preview Mode:

- Click **Dynamic Preview** on the **Hintline** toolbar. The button will be enabled when in Preview mode.

    To revert to Normal mode, click **Dynamic Preview** again.

While in this mode, any object can be manipulated or modified as if you are working in normal drawing mode, but what you're seeing is an accurate portrayal of your graphic to be exported.

14 Additional Information

Contacting Serif

Serif on the web	
Service and Support	www.serif.com/support
Serif website	www.serif.com
You Tube	www.youtube.com/serifsoftware

Additional Serif information

Main office (UK, Europe)	
Address	The Software Centre, PO Box 2000 Nottingham, NG11 7GW, UK
Phone	(0115) 914 2000
Phone (Registration)	(0800) 376 1989 +44 800 376 1989 800-794-6876 (US, Canada)
Phone (Sales)	(0800) 376 7070 +44 800 376 7070 800-489-6703 (US, Canada)
Customer Service	0845 345 6770 800-489-6720 (US, Canada)
Fax	(0115) 914 2020

For international enquiries, please contact our main office.

Credits

This User Guide, and the software described in it, is furnished under an end user License Agreement, which is included with the product. The agreement specifies the permitted and prohibited uses.

Trademarks

Serif is a registered trademark of Serif (Europe) Ltd.

DrawPlus is a registered trademark of Serif (Europe) Ltd.

All Serif product names are trademarks of Serif (Europe) Ltd.

Microsoft, Windows, and the Windows logo are registered trademarks of Microsoft Corporation. All other trademarks acknowledged.

Windows Vista and the Windows Vista Start button are trademarks or registered trademarks of Microsoft Corporation in the United States and/or other countries.

Adobe Flash is a registered trademark of Adobe Systems Incorporated in the United States and/or other countries.

Wacom, the logo and Intuos are trademarks or registered trademarks of the Wacom Company, Ltd.

Copyrights

Digital Images © 2008 Hemera Technologies Inc. All Rights Reserved.

Digital Images © 2008 Jupiterimages Corporation, All Rights Reserved.

Digital Images © 2008 Jupiterimages France SAS, All Rights Reserved.

Bitstream Font content © 1981-2005 Bitstream Inc. All rights reserved.

This application was developed using LEADTOOLS, copyright © 1991-2007 LEAD Technologies, Inc. ALL Rights Reserved.

Panose Typeface Matching System © 1991, 1992, 1995-1997 Hewlett-Packard Corporation.

The Sentry Spelling-Checker Engine © 2000 Wintertree Software Inc.

PANTONE® Colors displayed in the software application or in the user documentation may not match PANTONE-identified standards. Consult current PANTONE Color Publications for accurate color. PANTONE® and other Pantone trademarks are the property of Pantone LLC. ©Pantone LLC, 2012.

Pantone LCC is the copyright owner of color data and/or software which are licensed to Serif (Europe) Ltd. to distribute for use only in combination with DrawPlus. PANTONE Color Data and/or Software shall not be copied onto another disk or into memory unless as part of the execution of DrawPlus.

FontForge © 2000,2001,2002,2003,2004,2005,2006,2007,2008 by George Williams.

Portions of this software are copyright © 2008 The FreeType Project (www.freetype.org). All rights reserved.

Anti-Grain Geometry - Version 2.4 © 2002-2005 Maxim Shemanarev (McSeem)

TrueType font samples from Serif FontPacks © Serif (Europe) Ltd.

© 2013 Serif (Europe) Ltd. All rights reserved. No part of this User Guide may be reproduced in any form without the express written permission of Serif (Europe) Ltd.

Serif DrawPlus X6 © 1991-2013 Serif (Europe) Ltd. All rights reserved.

Companies and names used in samples are fictitious.

15 Index

Index

2D filter effects, 149
3D filter effects, 151
Actions tab, 170
Add (Join), 89
Add/Delete Pages, 24
adjustment (of pictures), 140
 fixing red eye, 141
Adobe Acrobat (PDF files), 189
airbrushes, 61
Align tab, 94
alignment
 of objects, 94
 of text, 70
animation, 165
 adding movies to, 173
 adding sound to, 172
 Autorun, 175
 exporting, 180
 Keyframe, 168, 173, 180
 Keyframe, previewing, 173
 onion skinning in, 167
 previewing, 168
 Stopframe, 166, 180
Arc Tool, 39
artistic text, 69
Artistic Text Tool, 69
audio clips (Keyframe animation), 172
augmenting, 87
Auto Connectors, 51
Autorun (Keyframe animation), 175
AutoTrace Studio, 136
AVI format, 180
Back One, 96
backgrounds (page), 14
banners, 12
Bevel & Emboss, 149
Bevel effects, 149
Bézier curves, 31
Bitmap fills, 107, 120
blend modes, 123
 colour, 123
Blend Tool, 155
blending
 colours, 123
 objects, 155
 on a path, 156
booklets (folded), 12
branches (connectors), 52
Bring to Front, 95
brush strokes
 applying, 63
 editing, 65
Brush Tool, 61, 63
brushes, 61
business cards, 12
Clipboard operations, 77
Clone Frame, 166
cloning, 78
closed lines (shapes), 34
CMYK, 14
 colours, 105
 JPEG export, 196
 palette, 114
 TIFF export, 196
colour models, 114
colour modes, 14
Colour Picker, 113
Colour tab, 104, 115
colours
 blend modes, 123
 defining, 115
 key colours (gradient fills), 119
 sampling, 112
 solid for lines and fills, 114
combining objects, 88
composite opacity, 127

conical fills, 116
connection points, 51
Connector Tool, 51
connectors, 50
    branched, 52
control handles (line editing), 48
Convert to Curves, 49
credits, 202
curved text, 74
curves
    drawing, 31
    editing, 43, 48
    filling unclosed, 34
    flow text on, 74
custom page setup, 12
cutout, 134
cutting objects, 77, 85
deleting pages, 24
dimension lines, 54
Dimension Tool, 54
dimensions
    setting units and scale, 20
distribution
    of objects, 94
Document Palette, 115
DPP format, 16
drawing scale, 20
drawings
    exporting, 192
    opening saved, 15
    perspective, 157
    RGB/CMYK, 14
    saving, 16
    start new, 12
drop shadows, 153
Dynamic Preview, 196
Easing tab, 170

editing
    brush strokes, 65
    connectors, 52
    curves, 43
    dimension lines, 57
    lines and shapes, 43, 49
    text, 70
editing curves, 48
effects, 123
    blends, 155
    curved text, 74
    envelopes, 158
    filters, 150, 151
    perspective, 157
    shadows, drop, 153
effects (images), 140
    PhotoLab, 139
ellipse fills, 116
Emboss effect, 149, 150
Envelope Tool, 158
envelopes, 158
EPS, 133
Erase Tool, 87
exporting
    animations, 180
    drawings, 192
    HD photos, 193
    multiple pages, 195
    objects, 191
    overlays, 194
    PDF files, 190
    Serif Metafiles, 193
    via Dynamic Preview, 197
features, new, 3
Fill Tool, 117, 120
Fill-on-Create, 34, 64

fills
- bitmap and plasma, 120
- changing, 118
- gradient, 107, 117
- mesh, 121
- solid, 106, 114

filter effects
- 2D, 150
- 3D, 151

filters, 140
folded documents, 12
fonts, assigning, 73
Format Painter, 80
formatting, text, 72
Forward One, 96
four colour fills, 116
frame text, 70
frames (Stopframe animation), 166
Frames tab, 166
Freeform Paint Tool, 88
gallery, 57
Gallery tab, 57
GIF, for animation, 181
Glow effects, 150
gradient fills, 107, 117, 118
Graphic Style Editor, 145
graphic styles, 145
greetings cards, 12
guides, 21
- ruler, 21

Guides Manager, 21
Hintline toolbar, 23
Image Cutout Studio, 134
importing pictures, 133
imposition in printing, 187
Inner Bevel effect, 150
Inner Glow effect, 150
Inner Shadow effect, 150
Insert Frame, 167
installation, 6
interface
- changing views, 23
- guides, 21
- page and pasteboard, 19
- rulers, 20

Intersect (Join), 90
Invert Selection, 29
Joint Tool, 176
Joints, 176
JPG (CMYK), 196
key colours (gradient fills), 119
key objects (Keyframe animation), 169
Keyframe Animation, 165
keyframes, 168
- changing duration of, 172
- inserting, 171
- object control in, 173

Knife Tool, 85
labels, 12
large documents, 12
layers, 96
- adding, 97
- deleting, 97
- locking, 98
- managing objects on, 98
- paper textures on, 98
- properties of, 98
- renaming, 97
- selecting, 97

Layers tab, 97
layout tools
- guides, 21
- page and pasteboard, 19
- rulers, 20

Line tab, 109
linear fills, 116

lines
    applying settings, 109
    closed (shapes), 34
    connectors, 50
    curved, 31
    defining colours, 116
    dimension lines, 54
    drawing, 29
    editing, 43
    extending, 31
    filling unclosed, 34
    reshaping, 45
    setting defaults, 109
    smoothing, 30
    styles for, 110
measurement units, 20
Mesh Fill Tool, 121
mesh fills, 121
metafiles, 133
modes (colour), 14
morphing (blends), 155
movies (Keyframe animation), 173
moving, 81
multiple pages
    exporting, 195
    printing, 187
multiple selections, 28
New Drawing, 12
new features, 3
Node Tool, 27, 36, 45
nodes, 45
    editing, 43
Nudge Distance (arrow keys), 81
objects
    adding to, 88
    aligning with each other, 94
    augmenting, 87
    cloning, 78
    combining, 88
    converting shapes to editable curves, 49
    copying formatting, 80
    copying, cutting, and pasting, 77
    cutting, 85
    deleting, 77
    distributing, 94
    editing bitmap and plasma fills on, 120
    editing gradient fills on, 117
    editing lines, 43
    editing mesh fills on, 121
    editing shapes, 43
    erasing, 87
    exporting, 191
    fills, 103
    grouping and ungrouping, 93
    joining, 88
    key (Keyframe animation), 169
    line settings, 109
    measuring, 20, 54
    moving, 81
    obstructive, 53
    on layers, 98
    ordering, 95
    outlines, 110
    QuickShapes, 35
    replicating, 78
    resizing, 81
    rotating and shearing, 83
    scale, 20
    selecting one or more, 27, 93
    selecting, in groups, 93
    splitting, 85
    storing in Gallery, 58
    tracing, 136
    transparency, 127
    tweened (Keyframe animation), 169

Index **211**

obstructive objects, 53
onion skinning (Stopframe animation), 167
opacity, 124
    composite, 127
Open (drawing), 15
ordering objects, 95
Outer Bevel effect, 150
Outer Glow effect, 150
outlines
    2D, 149
    brushes as, 110
    edge effects for, 110
page area, 19
page numbers and navigation, 23
Page Setup, 12
page units, 20
pages
    adding, 24
    backgrounds, 14
    deleting, 24
    exporting multiple, 195
    viewing, 23
palettes, 115
paper textures, 98
pasteboard area, 19
paths
    blending on, 156
    fitting text to, 74
PDF files
    previewing, 185
    publishing, 189
Pen Tool, 31
Pencil Tool, 30
perspective, 157
Perspective Tool, 157
photo brushes, 61
PhotoLab, 139
pictures
    adjusting, 139
    adjustments for, 140
    converting to vector format, 137
    cutting out, 134
    editing
        in PhotoLab, 139
    effects for, 140
    importing, 133
    importing multiple, 133
Pillow Emboss effect, 150
plasma fills, 107, 120
Pointer Tool, 27
posters, 12
pressure sensitivity, 65
Pressure tab, 66
previewing
    graphics dynamically, 197
    Keyframe animations, 173
    PDF files, 185
    Stopframe animations, 168
previewing (for print/PDF), 186
printing, 187
profiles
    pressure, 66
    printing, 188
Publish as PDF, 189
QuickShapes, 35
    adjusting, 36
    converting to editable curves, 49
    creating, 35
radial fills, 116
raster (bitmap) images, 133
    changing raster to vector, 137
Replicate, 78
resizing, 81
RGB, 14
    palette, 114
Rotate Tool, 27, 83

rotating objects, 83
rulers, 20
Run Forward (Keyframe Animation), 174
sampling (colours), 112
saving, 16
   animations, 166
Scalable Vector Graphics, 133
scaling
   of drawings, 20
   of line width, 111
selecting objects, 27
   invert selection for, 29
   multiply, 28
Send to Back, 95
Serif Metafile Format, 133
setup, animations, 165
Shadow Tool, 153
Shape Builder Tool, 88
shape text, 70
shapes
   combining, 88
   drawing, 29
   editing, 43
   joining, 88
   using QuickShapes, 35
shearing, 84
Size Objects, 81
small documents, 12
SMF, 133
Smoothness slider, 30, 47
solid colours, 115
solid fills, 106
sound (Keyframe animation), 172
Spiral Tool, 37
splitting, 85
spray brushes, 61
square fills, 116
stacking (ordering) objects, 95
Start New Drawing, 12
Start New Keyframe Animation, 165
Start New Stopframe Animation, 165
Startup Wizard, 11
stencils, 159
Stopframe Animation, 165
stopframes, 166
   cloning, 166
   inserting, 167
   onion skinning, 167
   reordering, 167
Storyboard tab, 169
Straight Line Tool, 31
stroke brushes, 61
styles (graphic), 145
Styles tab, 151
Subtract (Join), 90
support, 201
SVG/SVGZ, 133
Swatch tab, 105, 114, 118, 120, 122
system requirements, 6
tab
   Actions, 170
   Align, 94
   Brushes, 62
   Colour, 104, 115
   Easing, 170
   Frames, 166
   Gallery, 57
   Layers, 97
   Line, 109
   Pressure, 66
   Stencils, 159
   Storyboard, 169
   Styles, 151
   Swatch, 105, 114, 118, 120, 122
   Transform, 81

Transparency, 128
tags (gift), 12
technical drawings, 12
technical support, 201
text
   applying fonts to, 73
   artistic, 69
   converting to editable curves, 49
   editing, 70
   entering, 69
   flow on a curve, 74
   formatting, 72
   frame, 70
   retyping, 71
   shape, 70
three colour fills, 116
tint, 106
   adjusting, 106
Tool
   Arc, 39
   Artistic Text, 69
   Blend, 155
   Brush, 61, 63
   Connector, 51
   Dimension, 54
   Envelope, 158
   Erase, 87
   Fill, 117, 120
   Frame Text, 70
   Freeform Paint, 88
   Joint, 176
   Knife, 85
   Mesh Fill, 121
   Node, 27, 45
   Pen, 31
   Pencil, 30
   Perspective, 157
   Pointer, 27
   QuickShape, 35
   Rotate, 83
   Shadow, 153
   Shape Builder, 88
   Spiral, 37
   Straight Line, 31
   Transparency, 129
   Triangle, 41
tracing
   logos, 136
   photos, 137
tracing profiles, 136
Transform tab, 81
transparency, 127
Transparency tab, 128
Transparency Tool, 129
Triangle Tool, 41
tweened objects, 169
ungrouping objects, 93
vector bitmap, 136
vector graphics, 133
vector objects, 136
Weight of line (width), 111
zooming, 24